OUT OF DARKNESS

OUT OF DARKNESS
The Jeff Healey Story

CINDY WATSON

DUNDURN PRESS
TORONTO

Editor: Michael Carroll
Design: Jesse Hooper
Printer: Transcontinental

Library and Archives Canada Cataloguing in Publication

Watson, Cindy
    Out of darkness : the Jeff Healey story / by Cindy Watson.

ISBN 978-1-55488-706-4

1. Healey, Jeff. 2. Guitarists--Canada--Biography.
3. Blind musicians--Biography. I. Title.

ML419.H353W337 2010   782.42166092   C2009-907470-2

1 2 3 4 5   14 13 12 11 10

Conseil des Arts du Canada / Canada Council for the Arts

Canada

ONTARIO ARTS COUNCIL
CONSEIL DES ARTS DE L'ONTARIO

We acknowledge the support of the **Canada Council for the Arts** and the **Ontario Arts Council** for our publishing program. We also acknowledge the financial support of the **Government of Canada** through the **Canada Book Fund** and **The Association for the Export of Canadian Books,** and the **Government of Ontario** through the **Ontario Book Publishers Tax Credit** program, and the **Ontario Media Development Corporation.**

Care has been taken to trace the ownership of copyright material used in this book. The author and the publisher welcome any information enabling them to rectify any references or credits in subsequent editions.

J. Kirk Howard, President

Printed and bound in Canada.
www.dundurn.com

Dundurn Press
3 Church Street, Suite 500
Toronto, Ontario, Canada
M5E 1M2

Gazelle Book Services Limited
White Cross Mills
High Town, Lancaster, England
LA1 4XS

Dundurn Press
2250 Military Road
Tonawanda, NY
U.S.A. 14150

To Sherri, who fills my life with music and makes me believe I'm capable of anything.

CONTENTS

March 2, 2008: Legendary blues and jazz guitarist Jeff Healey has died.
— *CTV News*

Rock and jazz musician Jeff Healey died Sunday in a Toronto hospital after a battle with cancer. He was 41.... His unique playing style, combined with his blues-oriented vocals, earned him a reputation as a teenage musical prodigy.
— *Canadian Press*

Blind guitar wizard Jeff Healey of Toronto died Sunday of cancer. He was 41.
— *National Post*

Jeff Healey, arguably one of the most distinctive guitar players of our time, died today
(Sunday, March 2) in St. Joseph's Hospital, Toronto. He was 41, and leaves his wife,
Cristie, daughter Rachel (13) and son Derek (three), as well as his father and step-mother,
Bud and Rose Healey, and sisters Laura and Linda.
— *www.jeffhealey.com*

INTRODUCTION: YOU DON'T KNOW JACK ... I MEAN JEFF

I only met Jeff Healey once. He was already sick at the time, though I didn't know it. He didn't show it.

I picked my way down the dimly lit stairs to his Bathurst Street bar in Toronto that balmy June evening, waiting for my eyes to adjust, not sure what to expect.

"Don't worry," I was told. "You'll love him. He's as down-to-earth and approachable as you'll ever find."

They were right.

His easy laugh rang out as he worked the crowded room, making everyone feel welcome, important. Like magnetic north, he pulled all eyes to him. Not because he was flashy or pretentious — just the opposite. He was dressed for comfort, not show, with a muted blue shirt hanging loose over black jeans, the top two buttons falling open casually. Standing six feet two inches, he was taller than I'd imagined, with an air of physical energy surrounding him. A chunk of blond hair kept falling over his eyes, and he absently brushed it back with hands the size of footballs.

But for all his body mass, he was fluid. He carried himself with a quiet dignity and grace without even trying. A modern prince greeting his subjects, he remembered people he hadn't talked to for years, calling them by name as he recognized their voices. His voice was liquid gold.

And then he played. Transported to another time and place, he blasted out his powerful odes to life, and took the crowd with him. Experiencing his music altered me somehow. It hung in the air, surrounding me, as if I could almost touch it, a living thing. My senses awoke, heightened. At least, for the moment, life seemed more in focus.

Jeff Healey with Joe Rockman.

But none of that seemed as important as the man, the unstoppable force that was Jeff Healey. Given up for adoption as a newborn, losing both eyes to a rare form of cancer before his first birthday, suffering the return of cancer as an adult, losing his mother to breast cancer, Jeff Healey could have had all the excuses in the world not to succeed, to give up. But he chose to embrace each day, find the good in life, and squeeze every last drop of its juice to pour out for all of us to enjoy.

From three years old, when he first set a guitar across his lap, in what was to become his signature style, it was clear this was no ordinary kid. He loved music, loved to play, didn't let anything stand in his way. He cut record deals, made award-winning albums, travelled the world, hosted a radio show, and starred in a major motion picture, all by the time he was twenty-two years old.

Coming out of darkness, Jeff Healey created music, becoming one of the most influential Canadian musicians of our time. Refusing to use his blindness as a gimmick or marketing tool, he wanted to be recognized for his abilities, not his disability.

"I want to be known as a great musician, not a blind musician," Jeff said.

And he was.

PART ONE: GROWING UP

1

WELCOME
TO THE WORLD

March 25, 1966, snow dumps down in drifts in the biting cold. Clouds mask the stars; visibility is poor. A child is born, a boy, at St. Joseph's Hospital in Toronto. His first cry cuts the lonely night. But there is no celebration, no champagne corks popped. The father, a taxi driver, is probably not there at all. He may not even know about the boy. He is married, but not to the boy's mother. A sister lies sleeping at home, too, but she isn't dreaming about her new baby brother. She doesn't even know he exists. She never will. The birth mother is from a wealthy and well-known family in Hamilton, Ontario. She needs to keep this baby a secret.

And so Brian Alan Moody was placed in foster care without ever meeting his biological mother, father, or sister. Who could have guessed the future that was in store for this little bundle? He only had to wait three months for his family to choose him.

Baby Jeff in 1967.

2

THE CHOSEN ONE

Around the time Brian Alan Moody was born, in an apartment complex only a few minutes' drive from the hospital, Percival "Bud" and Yvonne Healey had started to think about adoption. They made a striking couple. At six feet four inches, firefighter Bud towered over Yvonne. Thick, dark hair framed a strong, square-cut face softened by golden-brown eyes that seemed to reflect the light when he looked down at his bride. She had to stand on tiptoe to reach his shoulder. Married eight years, they had no children. They had certainly tried. At thirty-two years old Bud figured it was time to consider other alternatives. Private adoption didn't work out, so they moved to Plan B. They weren't about to give up.

Imagine their excitement when they got the message at their Head Lake cottage, east of Orillia, Ontario, that early summer morning, July 18, 1966. Like most

Percival "Bud" and Yvonne Healey on their wedding day.

cottages at the time, there was no phone. Luckily, someone boated out to give them the news.

"Bud! Yvonne! A call came in for you. You need to call Children's Aid right away."

They wasted no time motoring over to the marina to place the call that would change their lives.

"It's a boy, Yvonne!" shouted Bud. "A boy is available. We can see him tomorrow."

The next morning they poured into their 1961 Pontiac, daring to hope this was the one. Was it their imagination, or did the sun suddenly seem to shine brighter that day? The drive back to the city was quiet, full of promise. In the driveway before heading inside to see the baby, Bud and Yvonne took a deep breath, glanced across the seat into each other's eyes, and squeezed hands. There was no reason to worry. When the baby reached his pudgy fists out to them, they fell in love at first sight. Ready or not, they were bringing their new son back to their two-bedroom apartment the next day, July 20, 1966. Three-month-old Brian Alan Moody became Norman Jeffrey Healey. He had found his home.

The smell of baby powder filled the apartment as the entire family rushed to meet this blond, blue-eyed gift. With seven aunts and uncles from Bud's side alone, and another aunt on Yvonne's side to coddle the new addition, it made for quite the welcome party. Jeff even peed on Grandma while she bathed him, a perfect golden rainbow arcing high into the air to mark the occasion.

"Welcome to the club," said Bud. "You've now received your official greeting."

After eight years of trying, Bud and Yvonne finally had a little bundle of joy to unleash their love on. Jeff had found a home where he would be loved completely, where he was meant to be.

Jeff Healey on Family

Judy M. Robinet, the executive director of the Windsor, Ontario, non-profit organization A Life Worth Living, quoted Jeff Healey's thoughts on family: "Today my family still takes precedence in my life. The values and traditions my parents passed on to me are valuable standards in all my day-to-day activities. First and foremost is their love. They daily demonstrated an immeasurable amount of devotion for one another. Secondly, even though I was adopted, I always felt an integral part of the family and was expected to fully participate in planned or spontaneous activities. They were a model for me in respecting people and in appreciating the value of a dollar. There were no broken promises — I could rely on their word. Finally, they always made time for me."

Jeff's parents, Bud and Yvonne, in May 1989.

The Healeys never thought of their family as different. They weren't a "lesser family" because it was formed by adoption.

"It's just like having your own child," Bud says. "A lot of people don't understand that."

Jeff obviously felt the same way. Shortly before his death, he said, as quoted by Deborah A. Brennan in her book *Labours of Love: Canadians Talk About Adoption*: "I can say completely, and to the end of my days, that concerning my life, everything that has happened, has happened for a reason. I was born and put here in the world for

Famous Adoptees

It's all the rage in Hollywood and the music industry to become an adoptive parent. Just look at Brad Pitt and Angelina Jolie. Three adopted kids, three birth kids, and rumour has it they're planning to shoot for ten. How many of those adopted children will go on to become famous in their own right?

Famous.adoption.com alphabetically lists more than seven hundred famous or influential people who were adopted, fostered, or otherwise "raised for a significant period during childhood by people other than ... birth parents." The list is intended to reassure adoptees "that they can aspire, that adoptees and fosterees have scaled the greatest heights of achievement, and that being adopted or fostered does not have to restrict one's attainments."

Here's just a sample of a few famous adoptees from past and present:

- Aristotle
- Dave Thomas
- Edgar Allan Poe
- Eleanor Roosevelt
- Faith Hill
- Jesse Jackson
- John Lennon
- Leo Tolstoy
- Malcolm X
- Melissa Gilbert
- Nancy Reagan
- Nat King Cole
- Nelson Mandela
- President Gerald Ford
- President Bill Clinton
- Priscilla Presley
- Ray Liotta
- Sarah McLachlan
- Tim McGraw

a reason. The people, who by the grace of God, were supposed to take care of me, adopted me. They were smart enough to recognize my health problems and get the help I needed. So I can very easily and justifiably say that adoption was the right thing for me."

Did Jeff feel any stigma about being adopted?

"I just thought that when you wanted a kid, all you had to do was make a phone call, talk to someone, and order one," he said, as quoted by Brennan in *Labours of Love.*

Jeff had no reason to feel any insecurity about his adoption. His parents were open and discussed the fact of his adoption from the time Jeff started talking as a toddler. It was a natural part of their family dynamic.

"If you ever get teased," his mother would say, "you tell them you were never rejected. You were chosen."

Jeff on His Dad

"I would say that every firefighter who worked in the Etobicoke Fire Department before 1990 knows who [Bud] Healey is. In fact, here in Etobicoke, I'm still *his* son, as opposed to him being known as 'Jeff Healey's dad.' And I'm very proud of that. He was and is memorable to those guys for very valid reasons. He is genuinely friendly, hard-working, and honest. What more can you ask for?"

Jeff and his father, Bud, in July 1969.

Jeff on His Mom

As quoted by Deborah A. Brennan in her book *Labours of Love*, Jeff had this to say about his mother, Yvonne, and his grandmothers: "My mother and grandmothers believe that I'm this special person who was put on this earth, different from the rest, for special reasons. Whatever I wanted to do, they defended and supported me. I always felt loved and cherished."

Quick Jeff Facts

Birth Name: Brian Alan Moody
Given Name: Norman Jeffrey Healey
Born: March 25, 1966
Died: March 2, 2008
Birthplace: Toronto, Ontario, Canada
Height: Six feet two inches
Eye Colour: Blue

Jeff and his mother, Yvonne in October 1991.

3

LIGHTS OUT

Was it a "happily ever after" story? Yes and no. Things were great in the Healey household for a while, but there were some bumps in the road in store for them. Bud and Yvonne Healey were thrilled with their new son, and by all accounts Jeff was a "good little guy." Everyone quickly settled into new routines. Bud came home from work each day as an Etobicoke firefighter, laid his six-foot-four frame on the couch, and perched his boy on his stomach for some quality time. Jeff giggled and gurgled as Bud played patty cake or fed him bits of sweet Macintosh apple. But one day, as the leaves were starting to turn red, orange, and yellow, Bud realized that Jeff only responded to his left side, only reached for the left side of the proud dad's face. He tried to catch Jeff's attention from the other side, wiggling his fingers or dangling bright toys, but it didn't work. There was no response.

Baby Jeff with his father, Bud.

A worried trip to the family doctor led them to a specialist and finally a diagnosis of retinoblastoma, a rare cancer of the eye. What a shock to the new parents! They experienced the typical range of emotional reaction, of course — fear, anger, confusion. But they didn't feel sorry for themselves. There was no "why me?" There was certainly no "we didn't sign up for this." They quickly focused on dealing with what needed to be done — what was best for Jeff. It was a little tricky because they were still in the trial period of the adoption; Children's Aid was technically Jeff's guardian. That didn't sit well with Bud.

"This is *my* kid," he said. "And *I* don't have the authority to give the doctors consent!"

There was no time to quibble; they had to move quickly to combat this aggressive cancer. The doctors suggested they remove one of seven-month-old Jeff's eyes, a terrifying prospect for the new parents. Imagine having to make the hard decision to cut your child's eye out. But it had to be done. The alternative was almost certain death. The medical experts concentrated on trying to save the other eye. Without laser surgery at the time, they used liquid nitrogen to freeze the tumour, but that didn't work, so at eleven months the doctors were forced to remove his other eye, as well. Baby Jeff's world went dark.

Remember that at the outset of this ordeal, Jeff was still in the probationary period of his adoption, so Bud and Yvonne could easily have sent him back. That suggestion shocks Bud. It never crossed their minds. He was their child. They loved him unconditionally.

Did you have a favourite stuffed animal when you were little? Did you take it to bed every night to keep you company in the dark? Just after Jeff's surgery, his parents got him a little stuffed toy — a crazy-looking purple-and-red cloth elf with a yellow plastic face. Jeff loved that elf. It stayed with him for years, even after he chewed most of its nose off. Especially at night, from their bedroom next door, his parents would hear Jeff call out, "Elf … Elf? Where are you, Elf?"

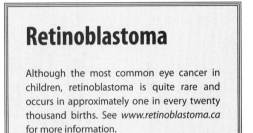

Retinoblastoma

Although the most common eye cancer in children, retinoblastoma is quite rare and occurs in approximately one in every twenty thousand births. See *www.retinoblastoma.ca* for more information.

They could hear the distress in his voice as they pictured him scrambling all over his crib, feeling around for Elf. Then the relief when he got hold of the toy. "Oh, there you are." Big sigh. "Hi, Elf."

Only then could Jeff drift off to sleep.

When Jeff learned to get out of his crib, he would feel his way out of the room, along the hall, and into his parents' room next door. Bud and Yvonne would sometimes wake to find Jeff standing next to their bed, listening to them breathe. It comforted him. The sound of their breathing would be as familiar to Jeff as your parents' faces are to you.

For quite a few years after the surgery, every time influenza or some other virus hit Jeff, Bud and Yvonne worried that the cancer was back. But as Jeff grew and flourished, they began to relax and dare to hope.

"Maybe it's not going to happen again," they told each other.

Bow-tied Jeff in 1971.

Childhood Cancer Until Age Fourteen

Approximately eight hundred and fifty Canadian children aged zero to fourteen develop cancer each year, but due to the successful treatment of the most common cancers, the number of deaths is one-sixth the number of cases. See National Cancer Institute of Canada, Cancer Statistics, at *www.cancer.ca*, for more information.

4

BIG BROTHER

After four and a half years as an only child, Jeff got a big surprise — twin sisters! Bud and Yvonne wanted to adopt a little girl, a sister for Jeff. They weren't looking for two, but when the call came in that ten-month-old twin girls were available, they decided to give it a try. What the heck? It wasn't as if they would have had control over everything if it was a natural birth. Besides, Bud was a twin himself.

Was Jeff jealous? Not a bit; he couldn't wait to get them home. Seat belts weren't mandatory in those days, so the proud big brother even got to carry one of his new sisters on his lap for their first trip home. They were still driving the same old 1961 Pontiac, but they had left the apartment that year for a new bungalow on Bonnyview Drive in Etobicoke. Just in time to make room for the twins.

Bud and Yvonne had already picked names for the girls, but Jeff staked claim first.

Seat Belts

Seat belts weren't mandatory in the 1960s, but safety-conscious Bud Healey retrofitted the back seat of his 1961 Pontiac himself to install home-designed seat belts for the twins' car seats.

He touched the creamy face of one, feeling her hot breath as his fingers brushed her lips. "This is Linda," he said. Then he patted the soft, dark curls covering the head of the other and smiled. "This is Laura."

And so it was.

How did Laura and Linda feel about having a blind brother? It was normal for them. They did everything sighted brothers and sisters do — even fight. Laura Healey has this to say: "Well, I guess with us growing up, always knowing he was blind, I never really thought that much about it. We just had to be really careful about not leaving anything out on the staircase. You had to push your chair in from the table. You couldn't leave any doors open. Mom and Dad were really strict on that. But I never really thought of Jeff being blind. If we wanted to go bike riding, Mom and Dad bought us a tandem bike, so he could ride with us. We went fishing together, or we'd play hockey on the street. To me he had no limitations."

In fact, if Jeff challenged you to a game of Scrabble or cards, you had to be prepared to lose. He was a killer Scrabble player and quite the card shark. But that didn't stop the twins from trying. They passed many hours taking Jeff's

Jeff with his parents, Bud and Yvonne, and his twin sisters in the early 1970s.

challenge as he sliced the deck. Watching cartoons was another favourite pastime, one that didn't involve competition. Jeff especially loved *The Flintstones*. Sitting cross-legged on the floor, he'd throw back his head and howl as Fred Flintstone and Barney Rubble got into another jam, or when Fred got ticked off and bellowed for his wife: *"W-W-W-Wiiiiillllllma!"*

> ## Try It On
>
> Think of your favourite game. What would you need to do or change to play it with someone blind?
>
> Try to come up with a list of games that can be played equally by blind and sighted children. What modifications or changes could you make to the games to make them accessible for blind playmates?
>
> Hint: Add a bell in a ball for soccer.

Do you have brothers or sisters? Do they drive you crazy? Do you think it would make a difference if they were blind?

For the most part, Jeff and his sisters got along well, but like most siblings they had their squabbles. The twins certainly didn't treat their big brother with kid gloves because he was blind. They admit they teased Jeff big-time. He hated vegetables, so they squashed parsnips and shoved them into his mashed potatoes, giggling while they hid the offending cream-coloured veggies. Jeff would take a bite, expecting Mom's fluffy, buttery, melt-in-your-mouth spuds, only to find bitter chunks to choke down.

He would spit out his mouthful and shout with outrage for the culprits. "Linda! Laura!"

The twins just had to make sure Mom wasn't around to catch them. Yvonne had gone to nursing school, but never actually practised the job after she met Bud. She was a full-time, full-on, stay-at-home mother. A tough taskmaster with the kids, she was especially strict with the girls. You would have thought she was running a boot camp sometimes. There were set outdoor playtimes, and the twins had to stay out for the duration, regardless of the weather. Dinner for the girls was served at exactly 5:00 p.m., ready or not. Yvonne was even known to poke around in the pot to find passable potatoes when they weren't quite cooked in time, rather than push back the girls' dinnertime by a few minutes. She wasn't so rigid with Jeff for some reason. And it wasn't pretty if Yvonne caught Laura and Linda picking on Jeff.

There was even more opportunity for the siblings to torment one another at the family cottage on Head Lake, where they spent the most time together as youngsters. After canoeing to the island, the tag-team sisters would wait until Jeff stood alone on the rocks by the blueberry patch. Once he was in position, they would yell, *"Snake!"*

It cracked them up to watch Jeff do the panic dance on top of the rock, trying to avoid an imaginary rattler.

Or riding the tandem bike uphill, the twins would quietly lift their feet off the pedals.

"Geesh, have you stopped pedalling?" Jeff would ask. "This is brutal. What's going on?"

Linda would smile and cross her fingers. "Nope, it's just a hill. Keep pushing."

Once, the dynamic duo took their brother by the arms, one on each side, Jeff's summer-white hair standing out in contrast to their mass of dark curls, like the filling in an Oreo cookie, and they walked him smack into a tree. *Umph!* Definitely not nice. Dad wasn't impressed. He knew they loved Jeff and meant it all in good-natured fun, but he was sputtering mad and determined to make the twins really think about what they had done. He made them both fumble around the cottage blindfolded for a day as a lesson after that escapade. That was one way to engender empathy.

But Jeff always got the twins back.

"It was unbelievable really," Laura says. "We'd try to hide and he'd come around the house and clap. He could sense if you were there or not. Then he'd grab us and throw us to the ground." Jeff used the vibrations and sounds bouncing back to zero in on the girls' locations. "I think he had, like, a tenth sense how he could pick up on things."

"What killed us," says Linda, "was we could sneak up on him and he would know which one of us it was. I mean, it didn't matter. He knew which one it was every time. We'd sneak up and he'd have his cane and — *whack!* right across the shins. He'd get us every time."

To make matters worse, Jeff never seemed to get in trouble. Yvonne and Bud were strict with the girls, but not so with Jeff.

"It was completely different," says Linda. "I didn't think it was fair. For instance, he got away with not eating his veggies, but Laura and I would be forced to eat ours. And he could have cookies that we weren't

Echolocation

Echolocation is the ability to sense objects in the environment by interpreting the sound waves reflected by those objects. People (or animals) create sounds, whether tapping a cane, snapping, or making clicking noises with their mouths. Using the echoes or sound waves bouncing off nearby objects, they can identify the location and general size of the obstacles.

Animals, including dolphins and bats, use a more sophisticated system of echolocation, since they can make sounds with much higher frequencies and rates, allowing them to echolocate to within a human hair's width!

allowed to have. He just had extra privileges. He could talk on the phone. We were limited on the phone. He didn't have curfews. We did. I thought we should have been treated equal. He got away with more."

Did Jeff really get treated differently, or was it just typical sibling rivalry, always thinking your brother or sister got more than you?

"No, Jeff definitely got more," recalls a close family friend. "We wondered sometimes. The girls couldn't have cookies or treats, but Jeff was always allowed. Poor Linda, especially. Sometimes it seemed she got blamed for everything."

When Linda grew up and moved out of the house, one of the first things she did was buy a bag of Oreo cookies and eat the whole thing herself — just because there was nobody around to tell her she couldn't.

Part of the differential treatment was probably because Jeff was four years older. It always burns to be a younger sibling and see your big brother or sister do things you aren't allowed to do. But also, for their early growing-up years, Jeff was away in Brantford, Ontario, midweek, at the W. Ross Macdonald School for the Blind, so the family only saw him on weekends. No doubt he scored a few extra treats to make up for lost time.

Linda, Jeff, and Laura in 1975.

Quick Jeff Facts

Jeff's Favourite Things: Cartoons, especially The Flintstones, Tasmanian Devil; chocolate cake; card games; Scrabble; Fudgee-O cookies; the cottage; turkey — he'd probably devour a whole one if he could; lasagna; Cheezies; Mars Food diner on College Street in Toronto.

Something Jeff Hated: Vegetables.

Places Jeff Hated: Anywhere that wasn't home.

5

YOUNG MUSICAL PRODIGY

Music always filled the Healey household; early jazz, big band, and dance music poured from the high-fidelity stereo. Before Jeff could even walk, he planted himself in its wake, holding the stereo to prop himself and rock to the music. He could barely stand, but he bopped to the beat. Jeff loved music from the start and fell into it naturally.

People talk about Jeff getting his first guitar at only three years old, but there are family photos of Jeff playing a mini piano even before that. As a toddler, he plopped in front of that little keyboard, smiling from ear to ear, pounding out music. While that piano is long gone, Jeff's first guitar hangs proudly on the wall, a reminder of how far he had come.

Bud played Hawaiian guitar as a young man, so he set up Jeff's first guitar the only way he knew how — as a Hawaiian, with the strings up high and a steel bar. Jeff

Toddler Jeff banging away on his mini piano.

was so small he couldn't hold the guitar on his lap, so he placed the instrument on the bed and stood beside it to play. The steel was a bit of a challenge, so an ever-curious Jeff took matters into his own hands, changing the guitar to regular tuning and bringing the strings down so he could push them with his little fingers. And so began Jeff's unusual style of playing.

His whole life people told Jeff he was "doing it wrong." He didn't care, though. Eventually, Jeff moved the guitar from the bed to his lap, laying the instrument flat on his knees, using his thumb as a fifth finger, playing up and down the frets like a keyboard to make great music. Plain and simple. Sure, it was unorthodox. But it worked.

Have you ever been told: "You're doing it wrong"?

Or "It just won't work"?

Did that make you want to quit?

There will always be naysayers in life, people who don't think outside the box, who believe if it hasn't already been done, it can't be. But if everyone bought that line, we would have no airplanes, no telephones, no electricity. Seem ridiculous? Well, it wasn't that long ago that some people still believed the Earth was flat, that if you walked too far, you would fall right off the edge into oblivion. It was also believed that the Earth stood still and the sun and other planets revolved around the Earth. Those beliefs were accepted as irrefutable facts until a few brave scientists dared to suggest their outrageous theories.

"Perhaps Copernicus was correct," said Galileo. "Let's determine if the Earth and other planets don't, in fact, revolve around the sun."

Poor Galileo. They said he was crazy. He stood trial for his views, was required to abandon support for the heliocentric view (the belief that the Earth revolved around the sun), was sentenced to prison, and had publication of his writing banned.

It takes courage to believe in yourself, to take risks, to follow your dreams, especially when everyone laughs at you or insists you've got it all wrong. It's a good thing Jeff Healey didn't pay attention to the critics, put down his guitar, conform, give up. If he had, the world would have missed out on a great musician.

Self-taught, at least at the outset, Jeff listened to

Hawaiian Guitar

While the origin of Hawaiian guitar music is generally credited to the Mexican and Spanish cowboys who were hired by King Kamehameha III around 1832, there is some debate over the origins of the Hawaiian steel guitar.

"Legend has it that in the mid-1890s Joseph Kekuku, a Hawaiian schoolboy, discovered the sound while walking along a railroad track strumming his Portuguese guitar. He picked up a bolt lying by the track and slid the metal along the strings of his guitar. Intrigued by the sound, he taught himself to play using the back of a knife blade." (Cited from *http://gohawaii.about. com/cs/hawaiianmusic/a/steel_guitar.htm*.)

Hawaiian guitar can be heard in blues, "hillbilly," country, rock, and pop music around the world.

The steel guitar is played differently than a traditional guitar. It's held in the lap, facing toward the player. The strings are raised above the fretboard. Rather than pressing the strings to the fretboard, a steel bar is pressed against the strings. The lap steel guitar is usually tuned to "open" rather than to standard guitar tuning.

music all the time and reproduced what he heard. But Jeff didn't know at first that recorded music had overdubbing, that even where only one guitarist was credited, there were multiple tracks of the same player overlaid on the records he took in. So, as he tried to capture all the sounds he was experiencing and absorbed each new song, his skills grew and grew. Soon he was able to mimic multiple lines of music at the same time.

Jeff loved Johnny Cash, a famous country music singer with a reputation as a bad boy. By the time Jeff was six years old, he had to rush out to grab each new Cash

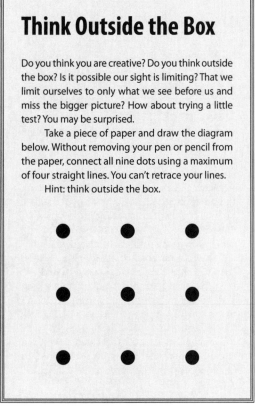

Think Outside the Box

Do you think you are creative? Do you think outside the box? Is it possible our sight is limiting? That we limit ourselves to only what we see before us and miss the bigger picture? How about trying a little test? You may be surprised.

Take a piece of paper and draw the diagram below. Without removing your pen or pencil from the paper, connect all nine dots using a maximum of four straight lines. You can't retrace your lines.

Hint: think outside the box.

album, inhale it in one sitting, and play back what he had heard with eerie accuracy. Jeff couldn't get enough. He would bang out what he heard on the radio, from albums, from church. When his Aunt Lucille played piano, Jeff would listen, head cocked to one side like a dog that had just caught the sound of something interesting. It only took ten seconds before Jeff picked up the tune to play alongside her.

His buddy, Glen Wade, recalls that "until Jeff was twelve years old, the heaviest music he would listen to was Elvis Presley."

"I remember Jeff singing 'Blue Suede Shoes,'" confirms "Uncle Lloyd," his father's best friend and old roommate. "Singing and bopping his head so forcefully, I thought it would pop off."

That was 1978. Everyone else was listening to Pink Floyd, Led Zeppelin, Queen, Elton John, and ABBA. Jeff was still listening to old jazz classics, big band, and country, with a little Elvis to spice everything up.

Not only could Jeff play the music, he knew the albums themselves by heart. It might be hard to appreciate today when we push a button to select our favourite music selections from our iPods or MP3s, but old record players had flat, circular pads (turntables), with small metal nubs in their centres. Record albums were flat black discs with small holes in their centres, barely visible grooves in circular patterns, and subtle, smooth spaces between each song. The album's hole fit the little turntable nub, the turntable would spin, and a tiny diamond chip at the end of a long arm acted

The Bell That Didn't Ring

Santa Claus is such a man,
He's got a big, big, belly.
When he laughs, it seems that it
Shakes like a bowl of jelly.
Gather round the campfire,
There's a story I want to tell
About Old Santa Claus
And his rusty old bell.
One dark and foggy night,
As the land was beginning to freeze,
He was going down to Pittsburg town,
And there came a little breeze,
It grew with every second
It blew harder than before.
Until, just like magic, One of the bells
Did not ring anymore.
Santa got out and looked around,
"My Goodness" he said with a sigh,
I guess that, That, One bell,
Just happened to say "Goodbye",
So since then, On Santa's sleigh
There has been one bell missing
Up until this day.

Composed by Jeffrey Haley.
(8 yrs. old.)

"The Bell That Didn't Ring": an early song by Jeff, composed when he was eight years old.

as a needle. Even with sight, it was very difficult to match the needle to the proper spot on the album, especially if you weren't starting at the first song. But Jeff could play any song from an album and set the needle down exactly at the beginning of whatever song someone requested.

It seemed as if Jeff could play anything he picked up. He taught himself to play guitar, piano, drums, trumpet, and trombone. His sisters looked on and sighed as they struggled with the recorder in grade school and Jeff picked it up off the table and made sweet, haunting music.

Jeff with an acoustic guitar in May 1979.

"Laura and I would suck," says Linda. "Then Jeff would just pick it up and be able to do it."

That was too much. Really, who can make a recorder sound good?

Bud and Yvonne wanted their musical prodigy to have formal training, so they signed him up for conservatory theory lessons in piano on Saturday mornings. Jeff hated it. He just wanted to play, to experiment. He would gladly play all day but didn't want to be bogged down with boring, regimented practice and theory.

Jeff also got bored playing country music early in his young career. He adored Johnny Cash and continued to love country music, but didn't find it challenging enough. Jeff felt that once you mastered a few basic chords you could play any country song. He wanted something more complicated, so he turned to jazz. Bud says he did so "because there's so much in jazz, there's a fill here and a fill there." Louis Armstrong and Duke Ellington were his idols. Jeff's approach to playing was different, probably in part because he wasn't influenced directly by other guitar players, but more by trumpet players.

When did Jeff start performing? He was used to playing to an audience at a young age. At eight Jeff and his dad stopped at the Dixie Flea Market in Mississauga, Ontario, where a man had a booth selling guitars. The man handed Jeff a guitar to try out, and within minutes a big crowd gathered to hear this kid play his unique brand of music. Jeff went back almost every weekend to perform at the market after that.

His television gigs began when he was seven. People from TVOntario approached Bud and Yvonne and asked them if Jeff could perform on one of their shows. Eventually, he appeared on TVO's *Cucumber* and *Kidsworld* and Hamilton CHCH-TV's *Tiny Talent Time* by the time he hit double digits. Jeff also played local fundraisers.

Around the same time, Jeff got a home mixing kit and began creating demonstration, or demo, tapes in the basement. He would disappear for hours at a time, alone downstairs, mastering track on track, dubbing and overdubbing, as he recorded his own harmonizing vocals and instrumentation. One of the first recordings of Jeff was as a preschooler singing "Shake, Rattle and Roll." Ironically, this was the final track on *Mess of Blues*, the last CD Jeff finished before his death, making the song his first and last recording. Was it intentional or coincidence?

Home Recording Studio

Ever think about cutting your own demonstration or demo CD? Why not? It isn't as tricky or mysterious as you might think.

If you are interested, head out to any good music or audio store and ask for help to get you set up with your first home recording studio. The store should be able to hook you up within your budget and give you some basic lessons on the how-to.

6

EYES ARE THE WINDOW TO THE SOUL

They say eyes are the window to the soul. What does that expression mean? Where does it come from? What if you have no eyes?

Jeff was fitted with glass eyes as an infant. A bright boy, he quickly learned how to flip them out. Like most toddlers, he had to put everything in his mouth. He used to pop them out and chew on them, soother-like, trying to fall asleep. That drove his mom crazy. Not only was it a choking hazard, but they were expensive — and not covered by health care back then. So, after good-night kisses, she would take out Jeff's glass eyes and leave them on the bedside table for morning. Just to give you some idea of the relative expense in terms of today's dollars, a single prosthetic eye today costs $1,500 — in other words, $3,000 a pair. That's an expensive chew toy!

Eyes Are the Window to the Soul

This well-known proverb is thrown around a lot, but what does it mean? It is generally used to suggest that someone's thoughts can be read by looking in his or her eyes, but there is a lot of debate over the origins of the phrase. Some believe it is a biblical reference, specifically Matthew 6:22–23 (King James Version):

> The light of the body is the eye: if therefore thine eye be single, thy whole body shall be full of light. But if thine eye be evil, thy whole body shall be full of darkness. If therefore the light that is in thee be darkness, how great is that darkness!

But many people disagree, since the biblical reference doesn't mention "window to the soul" in any of the translations.

The Random House Dictionary of America's Popular Proverbs and Sayings by Gregory Y. Titelman has this to say about the matter:

> The proverb has been traced back in English to "Regiment of Life" (1545). But the proverb was known much earlier. Cicero (106–43 B.C.) is quoted as saying "Ut imago est animi voltus sic indices oculi." (The face is a picture of the mind as the eyes are its interpreter.) The Latin proverbs, "Vultus est index animi" or "Oculus animi index," are usually translated as "The face is the index of the mind." The French say, "Les yeux sont le miroir de l'ame" (The eyes are the mirror of the soul). "The eyes are the window of the soul" is a variant form of the proverb …

Was Jeff embarrassed or awkward about his glass eyes? If he was, he never showed it. Always the prankster, he especially loved to take his eyes out on Halloween to freak out squeamish souls. His sisters' friends were the most likely targets. Getting a few squeals always brought Jeff's two-hundred-watt smile to his face.

Uncle Lloyd was one of the fainthearted. When Jeff tottered downstairs in the morning as a youngster waiting for his mom to put his eyes in, Uncle Lloyd cringed. He couldn't watch. For Jeff it was a natural part of who he was. He happily left his eyes out in a glass to soak for cleaning, for the world to see. There was no reason to be shy or self-conscious. Jeff was even known to flip out an eye and offer it up for inspection when meeting someone.

Have you ever been warned to quit playing so rough?

"Cut that out! Someone will lose an eye!"

Does that line sound familiar?

Well, in Jeff's case that caution was

more than a figure of speech; it was a reasonable concern. In fact, nine-year-old Jeff gave a whole new meaning to the old warning after wrestling with the Wilton boys at his parents' best friends' place in Flesherton, Ontario.

At some point, as the rambunctious boys tossed one another around the living room, one of Jeff's glass eyes popped out. The boys surveyed the room. "Oh-oh!" they all said.

It didn't take long to realize that the popular green shag carpet of the day wouldn't make for an easy search-and-rescue mission. Its deep pile could hide a secret army. It could certainly guard its new treasure — a clear, thin glass veneer with a blue-green tint. More like a glorified contact lens than the cat's-eye marble you might be picturing. Talk about finding a needle in a haystack!

"Mom, I lost an eye," Jeff finally came out to report.

Jeff's mom and Aunt Bea crawled across the carpet on hands and knees. They searched grid by grid for what seemed like ages, but even they had no luck.

Today Aunt Bea muses, "I still wonder if maybe his eye will turn up one day at the farmhouse."

Things to Think About

If forced to make a choice, would you rather be born blind or lose your sight later in life?

Most sighted people answer that they would rather lose their sight later, because they would be thankful to at least have the memories of some of nature's gifts of great beauty. There are answers like "I can't imagine not having ever seen ..."

But think about it. Do you really appreciate these visuals to the fullest? Or do you take them for granted? Do you stop to notice the way leaves dance when the wind hits them? The way they reflect light on a sunny day? Do you marvel at the whimsical spectrum of colours when a rainbow shimmers on the horizon, teasing us? How about the way snow lies heavy on the boughs of a tree just after a fresh snowfall?

Take a challenge. Every day for the next week, take a moment to stop and really notice some amazing visual that you encounter daily but might have ignored before.

While a number of blind people, when asked the same question, would like to have seen, to have memories of colour, to have those visual pictures stored, most said it was better to be born without vision, to learn the skills they need from the beginning.

"This is the way we see the world," said Andrea, a summer student at the Canadian National Institute for the Blind (CNIB). "I don't know any different."

Independent living-skills specialist Sumreen, who lost her sight after high school, said that while she is thankful she had the experience of sight, many who were born blind say if given the choice to get sight, they would prefer not. They believe it would be sensory overload.

PART TWO: SCHOOL'S OUT

7

DON'T GET SMART WITH ME

Was Jeff smart? Well, most people around him thought Jeff was born with a computer instead of a brain. It was as if he had a photographic memory. Musically, he clearly had an auditory photographic memory. But it went beyond that. As an adult, Jeff could still tell you where every single piece of furniture was in the first apartment where he lived — and he had left that place when he was three years old! He only had to be told a phone number once to remember it forever. His mind was a steel trap — a handy skill to have in school.

In later years Jeff had a collection of 78 rpm albums in addition to his many CDs. If you asked him for a song, he could pick the exact album you wanted out of his thirty-thousand-strong collection, feel the label, and tell you what side of the album it was on, the track number, and likely who played each instrument.

"It was like watching a magic trick," says Richard Flohil, Jeff's publicist. "I mean, how did he do that?"

But with genius often comes impatience. And while Jeff had boundless patience in some areas, in others he had none.

"Jeff didn't have great empathy for people not at his level," says bandmate Joe Rockman. "As with many great talents, as Jeff developed as an artist and person, he also developed a degree of intolerance for the shortfalls of himself and others. Jeff operated on a genius level in every way. It set him apart."

As a result, Jeff could be quite opinionated. He wasn't shy about being vocal about his opinions, either. If you were at the receiving end of one of Jeff's commentaries, no doubt he would seem unduly critical. His dry sense of humour sometimes came across as biting. While he usually had a solid basis to back up his position, he wasn't always the most tactful person. And because he was usually right, he tended to be extremely stubborn. Those skills served as a defensive cloak when Jeff was targeted in his later school years.

Things to Think About

Is it possible that Jeff's special talents and facility with numbers and directions were because of his blindness? If he was sighted, would his memory have been as sharp? Would his uncanny ability to replay something he had heard only once be as developed?

8

PRESCHOOL

Even as a young boy, Jeff was precocious. At two years old his favourite Christmas story was *The Night Before Christmas*. After a few reads, Jeff could recite the story aloud and turn the pages at precisely the right spot. When his cousin, Steve, who was three months older, came for a visit, two-and-a-half-year-old Jeff sat him down.

"I'm going to read this story to you," Jeff said.

He hopped onto the couch, opened the book, and proceeded to "read" to his stunned cousin, turning the pages as he went. No doubt poor Steve went home with a complex, convinced he was a slow learner by comparison.

At three years old Jeff went to Humber College Nursery School in Long Branch, Etobicoke. He did preschool for two years before graduating to kindergarten at Park Lawn Junior and Middle School in Etobicoke.

Is Your Classroom Ready?

What would you have to do to make your classroom ready for a visually impaired student? Try to come up with a list (individually or as a class exercise) of all the things you can think of that would ensure a safe and inclusive environment for a visually impaired student to participate in your class.

A few hints to get you started:

- Have tactiles on the back of the chairs to act as a nameplate for each student.
- Make sure chairs are tucked in.
- Put a bell on the soccer ball.

CNIB early intervention specialist Penny Smith points out that it is important to create an environment, both physically and emotionally, where the visually impaired student can say: "I'm not less than you. I just need you to do these things for me. I need you to make these small changes so I can contribute to your group. I'm not less than — just different."

But for Grade 1 he made the big move and switched to W. Ross Macdonald School for the Blind in Brantford, Ontario. His parents felt there was really no choice. He needed to learn specialized skills that he wouldn't get at a "regular" school.

9

W. ROSS MACDONALD SCHOOL FOR THE BLIND

Imagine that you are six years old … blind … starting Grade 1 at a new "residence" school, a live-in facility. You drive there with your parents (well, you don't actually drive yourself, but you get the idea) and quickly get caught up in introductions with a bunch of new playmates. You tear off to play in the sandbox, only to get up after a while and realize your parents are gone … but you're staying.

Are you still friends with your best bud from Grade 1? If so, do you expect to be lifetime friends? That was the case for Jeff with his pal, Glen Wade. The school year was already underway by the time Glen started at the W. Ross Macdonald School for the Blind in 1972. Glen's family had just moved to Ontario from Newfoundland. With one month under his belt, Jeff was experienced by contrast. Jeff befriended Glen and showed him the ropes about life in residence as a six-year-old. It took some adjusting.

There were six kids to a room. At 7:00 a.m. sharp the alarm sounded. Fifty kids, Grades 1 to 3, got up, got dressed, made their beds, and waited for inspection. Even the six-year-olds were expected to have perfect hospital corners and tightly pulled wrinkle-free sheets. If they passed inspection, they joined the silent lineup, waiting for breakfast. In the dining hall the sharp sound of a whistle warned everyone to settle down, the menu was announced, then all the kids had twenty to twenty-five minutes to eat before another whistle blew. Ready or not, it was time to leave. Everyone learned to eat fast.

W. Ross Macdonald School for the Blind

The W. Ross Macdonald School for the Blind opened in Brantford, Ontario, in 1872. The school was originally called the Ontario Institution for the Education of the Blind. Subsequently, it was known as the Ontario School for the Blind. The name was officially changed to W. Ross Macdonald School in 1974 in honour of Brantford citizen W. Ross Macdonald, who served as lieutenant governor of Ontario from 1968 to 1974.

Jeff and Glen became best buddies, a friendship that was to last a lifetime. Roommates for six out of seven years at W. Ross Macdonald, they both loved practical jokes. In fact, Jeff bore scars from Glen's pranks throughout his whole life. Horsing around in Grade 3, Glen tripped Jeff. No big deal. It was all in fun; they had done it to each other loads of times. This time Jeff split open his chin, but a few stitches later he was raring to go. Glen got a little more daring in Grade 5. He set a metal garbage can on top of their shared bedroom door. He had wanted to fill it with water, but luckily someone talked him out of it. As it was, the empty can did enough damage. With the trap in place, Glen called his bait.

"Jeff! Hurry! Come to the room!"

On cue Jeff came barrelling in. The second he pushed open the door the metal garbage can dropped onto his head. He knew it was Glen right away and pulled the culprit to the ground. They wrestled around on the floor until Glen realized something was wrong.

"Hey, Jeff, something's not right. I feel something warm and sticky."

Sure enough, Jeff's head was split open, and it was off to the hospital for stitches again.

But through all the scrapping, they looked out for each other. Jeff was always top of the class; he especially loved reading. Glen did not. So Jeff always obliged by giving him the Healey "Cole's Notes" version of their required reading books.

How does Glen describe Jeff as a friend? "Loyal, caring, a great listener, always going the extra mile and a half, someone you could depend on."

Glen was one of Jeff's few close friends who wasn't involved in music, though Jeff did play guitar from the time Glen first met him.

In fact, Jeff started his own radio show for his Grade 3 classmates. Someone brought in a cordless microphone, which Jeff tuned into a favourite radio station frequency, introducing the music as the dormitory's official DJ.

Fascinated with music and sound, Jeff couldn't get enough. He loved to experiment, trying to find new sounds and sound effects. Regularly, he roped in his partner in crime to help out. According to Glen, they went through a lot of microphones during this experimental phase. Not surprising, since Jeff threw them downstairs, trying to create new and unusual effects in his recordings.

Look Through Their Eyes: CNIB Simulator Kits

The Canadian National Institute for the Blind (CNIB) has simulator kits available. See the CNIB's website at *www.cnib.ca*. The kits include special glasses that simulate the experience of someone visually impaired. In other words, you could try on glasses that let you experience what it would "look" like through the eyes of someone with tunnel vision, or floaters in front of their eyes, or cataracts, or maybe even one eye missing. Pick a pair and try them on for size for part of a day. Imagine yourself as someone with that visual impairment. The simulators will allow you to briefly "look through their eyes."

Consider trying this as a class project at school.

Eight-year-old Jeff even initiated his first band at W. Ross. He played guitar, of course, recruiting his Grade 3 buddies to play drums, sticks, whatever they could muster. Glen got to play tambourine.

"That's about as musical as I got," says Glen. He recalls Jeff always looking for ways to express himself. "He never let anyone tell him he couldn't do anything. If he wanted to do something, he figured out a way to do it."

In the school's music program, Jeff started out on trombone, but he didn't like it much, so he switched to trumpet, an instrument he would come back to later in life.

Outside of music, mathematics was Jeff's favourite subject. That's not so surprising when you consider how good Jeff was with numbers. After he learned to use an abacus at W. Ross Macdonald, his dad would test him, giving him columns of three-digit numbers to add. While Bud was just putting the line under the numbers to begin adding, Jeff would already be announcing the answer.

If you gave Jeff a date months down the road to schedule something, he would say, "September 9, well, that will be a Tuesday," as if retrieving the data from the hard drive of his brain, as if the calendar pages appeared full-blown in his mind. Likewise, if you talked to him about an event that happened years ago, Jeff could say with absolute accuracy, "Yeah, I remember that party. It was on a Thursday night. What a blast!"

Consider the thousands of songs Jeff knew, sang, and played. It's remarkable to think that he never saw a written word or note, but learned everything by ear.

Try This On

How about trying a game of scavenging that blind and sighted kids can enjoy alike — a sensory scavenger hunt? Instead of listing items to find that rely on sight, it's easy to modify the game to list items that invoke your other senses: touch, smell, and hearing.

Sensory Scavenger Hunt

Can you find ...
- Something that's prickly?
- Something that has a pleasant smell?
- Something that does *not* have a pleasant smell?
- Something that's rough?
- Two different types of tree bark?
- Something that's squishy?
- Something that's smooth?
- Something that's soft?
- Something that's hard?
- Something that makes a loud sound?

BONUS!
Find something you've never found before!

Things to Think About

Did you know that you are likely to perform better on tests, particularly in mathematics, if you study music?

Numerous studies have been conducted in recent decades, and the consistent results suggest that students who play piano, or have other musical training, perform significantly higher on tests of fractions and proportional math than those children who do not. Studies have targeted kids from preschool age to university entrance scores, and the results have supported the theory at every level.

10

GRADE 8 – TRANSITION YEAR

Grade 8 was a tough year for Jeff, a transition year. His parents decided to transfer him back to "regular" school, so he joined his younger sisters at Park Lawn Junior and Middle School for his last year of elementary education. Many of the kids didn't understand him, didn't accept him, and targeted him because he was different. He was blind. He was smart. And he was musically talented.

It was a lonely year for Jeff. Pulled away from familiar routines, surroundings, and friends he had made over the past seven years, he was tossed into an environment where he was singled out and tormented. Jeff was followed home from school, taunted, tripped, and beaten up while his younger sisters looked on helplessly or tried without luck to intervene. I wonder what those bullies thought when Jeff's albums went platinum?

Jeff didn't want to be treated differently. Even when he finally fought back at Park Lawn, after taking months of bullying, Jeff was upset that the instigator was punished, but he wasn't.

"I was in the fight, too," he said at the time. "Why would he get punished and not me? Don't treat me any different because of who I am."

His constant companions during that rough year were his two pet guinea pigs, Archie and Munchie.

"They were the loves of his life," says his sister, Laura. "It's sad to say, but I think they were his best friends at one point, because of that transition from the blind school to the sighted school. Munchie would lie on the bed with him, and they'd just listen to music. When Munchie died, Jeff was devastated."

It seems we humans could learn a lot from our animal friends about unquestioning acceptance, love, and loyalty.

Things to Think About

Have you ever picked on someone because he or she was different? Try to think of a time when you might have hurt someone who didn't deserve it. Can you replay the incident in your mind? Bring back as many details as you can about what you said or did and how the person reacted. Then try to imagine yourself in that person's shoes. Relive the entire scene, but with yourself cast as the "victim." What would your reaction have been? Now consider writing an "I'm sorry" note or letter to the person. Or maybe go out of your way to do something special for him or her.

11

HIGH SCHOOL

Grade 9 was easier for Jeff. He started at Etobicoke Collegiate Institute with the other local Grade Niners. Jeff was still the only blind kid in the school, but he had his music. It was like communicating in another language. Besides, he had his guitar, a shield between him and the world.

"People still weren't too sure of him," says Laura, "but then they found out, 'Wow, this guy can really play music.' They accepted him better."

Not worried about being part of the "in crowd," Jeff didn't care about following the fashion trends of the day. He hung out with people who interested him, not caring if others thought they were quirky. He was never a follower. If people didn't get him or didn't think he fit in to their pigeonholed categories, he wasn't going to lose any sleep over it. He had his music.

Jeff got involved in every music program he could, playing lead guitar in the band for dramatic musical productions (school plays), performing in the Etobicoke Collegiate school band, playing in a school jazz band, and competing in the Canadian Stage Band Festival. He was focused on his music; he was intense.

"Every day, every chance he got, he was playing guitar," says his father. "The music was his, and that's what he concentrated on. The music really took over."

Not surprisingly, Jeff won the Board of Education Award for Excellence in Music at Etobicoke Collegiate. And he blew everyone away when, at only fourteen, he acted as the principal music specialist for the Canadian Broadcasting Corporation (CBC), with a weekly radio broadcast in which he aired vintage selections from his 78 rpm album collection.

Things to Think About

As a young boy, Jeff sat for hours on the front step of his grandmother's house in St. Thomas, Ontario, strumming his guitar. He didn't know it, but across the street a woman would open her windows to listen. Her son-in-law, Paul Mills, just happened to be a producer with CBC Radio.

"You should come and hear this boy play," she would say to Paul. "He's really quite good. Maybe you could do something for him."

Paul never got the chance to come and hear young Jeff play. But years later Jeff came to work for CBC Radio on his own.

Do you think some things in life are just meant to be?

Jeff's Board of Education for the City of Etobicoke Certificate of Award.

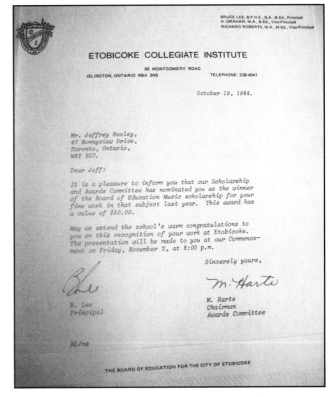

Music scholarship letter from Etobicoke Collegiate.

On top of that, Jeff put together his first serious band, and in his high-school years was already starting to play gigs wherever he could. By his mid-teens, he was being hailed as a musical prodigy.

Jeff didn't have the support of his sisters through his high-school years. By the time the twins hit secondary school, Jeff was already gone. Maybe that was just as well. With a four-and-a-half-year age spread, "Jeff was a teenager, so it wasn't cool to hang around your younger sisters," his sisters say.

But that didn't stop Jeff from being a protective big brother.

"If Dad was working nights and there was a storm or something, I'd be so glad Jeff was home," says Laura. "I felt so protected when he was there. I remember waking up as a kid at night and thinking, *Oh, am I glad Jeff's here.*"

Ticket for the Tenth Annual Canadian Stage Band Festival National Finals.

Other times Laura and Linda weren't so glad he was protective. Sometimes it could be a royal pain, like when they brought boys home. Jeff's protective nature wasn't necessarily so great then. The girls knew their brother would check out their potential dates and give the guys a hard time. It's tough enough bringing home a crush without your big brother busting his chops.

On the crush front, Jeff never hurt. Maybe it's true that women love musicians, because Jeff's romantic life kick-started in high school.

"There was a parade of women," says Linda. "It started, I'd say, from Grade 11, and continued right along. He never suffered in that respect."

Laura echoes the sentiment. "Oh, my goodness … he just seemed to have a slew of them. Oh, my goodness … very much so. He was quite the charmer."

But the one girl the Healey family hoped Jeff would hook up with remained his constant friend. Karen Johnson befriended Jeff in Grade 8, and they remained friends throughout their high-school years. Later Karen kept in touch even after moving to Halifax, Montreal, and finally California.

Did he ever get his heart broken?

"I think he did most of the heart-breaking," says Laura. "I don't remember anybody ever breaking his heart. He always seemed to have somebody else lined up. That was about the only thing that bothered me about Jeff. Probably from the age of fifteen on he was never alone." Otherwise "he was very thoughtful and very sensitive of other people's feelings."

The Premier
of Ontario

Parliament Buildings
Queen's Park
Toronto, Ontario
M7A 1A1

965-9353

June 28, 1983

Dear Jeff:

It has come to my attention that you were recently selected to be a member of the All Star Band at the 11th Annual Canadian Stage Band Festival National Finals.

This was a well deserved recognition of your talents and abilities and I am sure your parents and teachers share with you the pride and satisfaction you must feel in having earned this honour.

This Festival offers a unique educational and broadening experience for Canadian youth who share a common bond through their love of music, as well as an opportunity for public performance.

I congratulate you on your dedication to music, thank you for sharing your talent, and convey the hope that music will continue to bring you much joy and pleasure throughout your life.

Sincerely,

Bill Davis

William G. Davis

Mr. Jeff Healey,
Etobicoke Collegiate Institute,
86 Montgomery Road,
ISLINGTON, Ontario.
M9A 3N5

Letter from Ontario Premier Bill Davis congratulating Jeff on his selection to the Eleventh Annual Canadian Stage Band Festival National Finals.

65

12

IS THERE LIFE AFTER HIGH SCHOOL?

Bud Healey wanted Jeff to be a lawyer, convinced that with his steel-trap mind his son would be a sure success. The music industry was difficult and unpredictable. Bud wanted Jeff to have something solid to fall back on. But Jeff's passion was music, and he couldn't ignore its call.

Jeff was awarded a scholarship to go to Humber College for music. Strings had to be pulled, since he was still technically a few credits shy of his Grade 12 diploma. Although very smart, Jeff let extracurricular music activities and late-night gigs cut into his study time. He tried college for a while but had to make the hard decision whether to stay in school or pursue his career in the tough music industry right away. Jeff felt he already knew more than many of the courses could offer. Besides, about that time, a buzz had started: he got noticed by some big names in the music business when he played Grossman's Tavern and Albert's Hall in Toronto. He decided to leave school. At first his parents were disappointed, but things fell into place quickly for Jeff after that, and like a prize racehorse at the Kentucky Derby, his career took off.

Ironically, Jeff was awarded a doctor of letters by McMaster University in Hamilton, Ontario, in June 2004. Jeff appreciated the honour but found it amusing, since he hadn't really finished high school. "Dr. Healey" even got an official McMaster school tie as an extra perk.

Jeff at the ceremony where he received his doctor of letters at McMaster University.

Notice of McMaster University's conferral of a doctor of letters on Jeff on June 3, 2004.

Jeff was also awarded an Honorary Licentiate in Music by Conservatory Canada in November 2007. He was too sick to attend the event by that time, though, so he asked his father to accept the honour in his place.

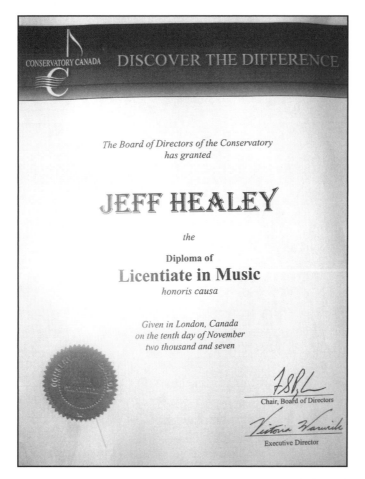

Conservatory Canada's Honorary Licentiate in Music awarded to Jeff in November 2007.

PART THREE: MAKING MUSIC

13

FIRST BAND: BLUE DIRECTION

Not counting his Grade 3 musical experiments, Jeff started his first real band when he was still only in high school. The four-piece group briefly toyed with a trial name but finally decided on Blue Direction (a pretty cool name), with Jeff on lead guitar, schoolmate Rob Quail playing second guitar, Jeremy Littler on bass, and Graydon Chapman on drums.

Rob Quail remembers the first time he met Jeff. Actually, he heard Jeff playing before he saw him. Fifteen-year-old Rob had been invited to a pajama party, the kind where there was probably going to be some underage drinking. He didn't know it, but Jeff, thirteen at the time, had been invited, too. Rob had just taken up guitar shortly before and was hooked, so when he heard there might be a chance to jam, to improvise with other music lovers, he grabbed his guitar and strapped it on for the ride.

When he stepped into the house, he wasn't disappointed. The sound of a steaming-hot guitar solo filled the place. Excited, Rob followed the music, drawn like a rat after the Pied Piper. Who could be playing? It must be someone's dad, a professional. No one their age could play like that. This wasn't just someone playing his instrument. This was someone making music. It made you feel. There was real emotion. It didn't take long to find the room where the impressive sound flowed from, but Rob was distracted by a kid sitting in the corner with a guitar flat across his lap. It was obvious the kid was blind. Rob was drawn to him. It took a few moments before he clued in that the music was coming from this blind, blond dynamo. But how was that possible?

Jeff and Rob became close friends and bandmates. Rob acknowledges that he wasn't nearly as proficient as Jeff, but Jeff loved energetic and passionate players. Rob fitted that bill. The duo hooked up with two buddies, and Blue Direction was born.

Rob doesn't remember Jeff ever practising. "Jeff was genetically engineered to make music," he says. "It was incredible. It ticked you off sometimes. He had a photographic memory for sound. He remembered every note."

Distinctly, Rob remembers driving his mom's Toyota Tercel, with Jeff in the front seat and the other two bandmates piled into the back. It was 1979. Rob had just gotten his driver's licence. Van Halen's hit song "Jump" came on the push-button AM radio. It was their first time hearing it. They went crazy in that cramped car. When they got to the rehearsal hall, the guys were still pumped, raving about the song.

"We should go get the record. Maybe we could learn it. We should give it a shot."

Jeff sat down without saying a word, took out his guitar, and played the song. Perfectly.

So they had a decent band and a catchy name. But how to go about getting gigs? They had no idea.

"We would just go to a club and ask for the owner," recalls Quail. "Then we played until he hired us."

As the name Blue Direction implies, they played mostly blues-based music, but also pop material by the likes of Eric Clapton/Cream, John Cougar, Chuck Berry, The Beatles, Phil Collins, and Bruce "The Boss" Springsteen. Jeff also knew the old rock-and-roll stuff by Dion and the Belmonts, Elvis Presley, and Jerry Lee Lewis, so sometimes they would pull a tune by one of those musicians out of the hat at a gig. The band even tried on a handful of originals, including three or four songs they had each written separately and a couple Jeff and Rob Quail had composed together.

"In fact," recalls Quail, "the guitar riff at the start of 'My Little Girl' from *See the Light*, the first Jeff Healey Band album, is almost identical to the 'hook' from an original instrumental song we came up with together, called 'Turn It Down.'"

"Turn It Down" got its name when the boys were rehearsing in Jeremy Littler's basement and his parents kept calling that plea down the staircase.

"Turn it down! Please! Could you just turn it down?"

"Adrianna" was one of the original songs the band played in those early years. It was also the first 45 rpm record The Jeff Healey Band ever pressed.

Blue Direction split up in 1983 or 1984, but Jeff and Rob played together in the first lineup of what was already being booked as The Jeff Healey Band.

At The Jeff Healey Band's first public appearance it attracted enough attention to warrant a write-up in the trendy Toronto arts and entertainment magazine *NOW*. Jeff was young. He was outrageously talented. He was blind. He played in an "unorthodox" manner, guitar slung on his lap, thumb used as a fifth finger. How could he not get noticed?

Jeff's publicist, Richard Flohil, loves to tell the story of the talent scout who came to check out Jeff perform at Toronto's Grossman's Tavern, a breeding ground for blues-based bands then and now.

The scout is reported to have said, "Look, there's no future in this blues crap at all, and the kid needs a gimmick."

Flohil laughs. "This is one of those stories that ranks with the poor unfortunate man from England who decided not to sign The Beatles because the train fare from Liverpool would be more than signing The Tremeloes, who only had to come from Essex."

The modern literary equivalent might be the bad judgment call of the editor who turned down J.K. Rowling's first Harry Potter manuscript, telling her there was no market for wizard books. Hindsight is always 20/20. We all make decisions at some point that we spend the rest of our lives kicking ourselves over.

But in the fall of 1984, when Jeff was eighteen, a buddy named Cory asked him to come and check out one of the great all-time bluesmen.

"Hey, Jeff, Albert Collins is playing Albert's Hall. Let's check it out."

"Nah," said Jeff.

"I'll buy you a beer," said Cory.

"Okay."

A few hours later Cory had convinced Albert Collins to allow Jeff onstage to jam with him. Collins was blown away. He invited Jeff to come back that Saturday when legendary blues guitarist Stevie Ray Vaughan would be playing. So Rob Quail sat in the crowded bar a few nights later, thrilled to watch his friend and bandmate jam with Collins and Vaughan.

"The only way to describe the look on Stevie Ray Vaughan's face was gob-smacked," says Quail.

"Gob-smacked? What's that?"

"Absolutely blown away."

Collins and Vaughan were considered "greats" in the music industry. It took a serious talent to make them sit up and take notice. Jeff had plenty of that.

"Any venue I ever played with Jeff," recalls Quail, "people just went crazy. He was so talented … so unique … we killed it. Jeff always took performing seriously. It didn't matter if he was playing to a half-empty room or to a packed concert hall. He always put all of his heart and soul into a performance."

14

THE JEFF HEALEY BAND

The Jeff Healey Band initially featured Jeff, Rob Quail, bassist Terry Murphy, and a series of drummers, the last of whom was Tom Stephen. They had landed a Wednesday night house gig at Branko's, a smoky, dark, dive of a bar at Bloor Street West and Lansdowne Avenue in Toronto, and they were finally getting opening gigs for higher-profile acts such as Robert Cray and Albert Collins.

Somewhere along the way Stephen decided that a trio was the way to go, and in late 1985, when they were looking for a new bassist, he called Joe Rockman. "Have you ever heard of Jeff Healey?"

"Yeah," said Rockman, who had just read an article about Jeff. "He sounds interesting."

"Well, I've hooked up with Jeff," said Stephen. "I'm playing drums with him."

There was a pause at the other end of the line.

"Really?" Rockman finally said.

Stephen asked if Rockman wanted to be the band's bassist. Joe was unsure; Jeff was nineteen, Rockman was twenty-nine, with his own gig going and a full lineup for the upcoming Christmas season. Tom trusted Rockman's experience and wanted verification that Jeff was the real thing.

And so Joe Rockman headed out for a meeting that would change the course of his life. He figured it wouldn't be a loss either way. The joy of the music at Grossman's famous Sunday night jams was always worth the trip. As he entered the dim and dingy bar, the smell of beer filled his nostrils, and the familiar din of musical instruments crammed his ears. Jam nights were chaotic, with everyone jostling for a prime spot. Usually, you had to play with whoever you got hooked up with, but Tom Stephen had convinced the coordinator to let the three of them play together that night — an audition of sorts for one another.

Rockman didn't know what to expect, but as soon as Jeff stood to shake his hand, he "instantly knew Jeff had the equipment."

"Jeff had the longest fingers of a white man I'd ever met," Rockman says. "He could put his little finger at the nut, and his thumb could reach the twelfth fret. And there was something else there. He had a presence, an aura of quiet power, an air of understated confidence, a degree of insecurity and vulnerability — all the tells of a great artist."

It didn't take ten seconds of playing together for Joe Rockman to know they clicked. "It wasn't on the surface of the notes. It was between the notes. It wasn't the way he played guitar, but the way he played music. It was behind it and underneath it. I instantly knew what to do on bass to support it. It was the kind of thing a guy like me could only dream of."

And so the trio that hit the fast track to fame, becoming world-renowned as The Jeff Healey Band, was born. The problem was that nobody had bothered to tell Rob

Quail. He showed up at their Wednesday night Branko's gig, only to have Jeff tell him, "Sorry, but Tom's decided we'd be better off as a trio." That had to hurt.

For Rockman, though, it wasn't that first performance that made him commit. It was their third gig together at the Brunswick House on Bloor Street West in Toronto, playing before a crowd drinking beer out of pitchers. The performance was taped, so Rockman had the chance to listen to it later, objectively, when he wasn't caught up in the moment of creating. He can remember the exact moment when he was hooked.

There's no way a guitar player, playing conventionally, could do that, he thought.

Joe had to replay the piece a few times.

Have you ever seen the Road Runner cartoon? Well, picture the Coyote when he skids to a stop and his jaw hits the pavement. That was Joe Rockman as he replayed Jeff's guitar solo. Not surprising — Jeff was known for his improvisational solos, for taking a road map but finding his own way to get there.

"Listening to what Jeff was saying," recalls Rockman, "there was a Jimi Hendrix and Eric Clapton influence, but what came out was so much larger than that. Jeff added his own dimension of Louis Armstrong and created a whole new dimension. I threw away my studio contracts — everything — to take a chance on this moment."

At first the band was turned down by every record company in Canada. "Canada saw us as a successful bar act," says Rockman. "We knew we were more than that."

Luckily, they were one of the few Canadian groups able to sign directly with a U.S. company. Things fell into place quickly for the band after that, with a whirlwind of attention, including a record deal; the hit single "Angel Eyes"; the platinum album *See the Light*; magazine covers; and CASBY, MuchMusic, Grammy, Juno, and Toronto Music Award nominations and awards. Then came Patrick Swayze in the hit 1989 movie *Road House*, with The Jeff Healey Band performing on-screen and providing the music. The film and soundtrack garnered even more public attention, adding to the Healey hype that was sweeping the music industry.

It must have been difficult for Jeff's parents. Their boy was suddenly on the road touring the world. But they could see his face plastered across newspapers, magazines, posters, and concert and album advertisements. However tough it was on his parents, it was an interesting and challenging time for Jeff. He had to learn the ropes quickly; it was trial by fire. Once The Jeff Healey Band was cast in *Road House*, there was no time for reflection on the explosion of the group's career. Jeff and his bandmates woke up at 4:00 a.m., fought Los Angeles rush-hour traffic in their rented van, hit the movie set by 6:00 a.m., and put in twelve-hour days shooting the flick. Evenings were spent at the recording studio, trying to get perfect takes for the *Road House* soundtrack, or for the band's first CD, *See the Light*.

Advertisement for Toronto Music Awards in 1987. The Jeff Healey Band was nominated in the Best Toronto Blues Group/ Artist and Best Toronto Club Band categories, winning in the first one. Jeff himself was nominated in the Toronto "Rising Star" Guitarist category, which he won, and he also co-hosted the awards ceremony.

Jeff's sisters were thrilled when The Jeff Healey Band was featured in *Road House*.

"From the time Jeff was little, we'd be dragged off to see him play, so that was just normal," says Linda. "The only thing that was really good was when he played with Patrick Swayze. That was, like, wow!"

Dirty Dancing had just been the hit summer movie not long before. Patrick Swayze was considered *hot, hot, hot*. He was the poster boy hanging in many a young girl's bedroom.

While Linda may have fond memories of meeting the hottie Swayze, she carries one of those red-faced-moment memories right beside it. The sixteen-year-old twins were allowed to skip school, travel to California, and sit in on the set to watch the filming of *Road House. Hollywood here we come! How cool is that?*

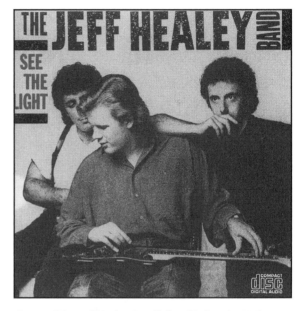

Cover of The Jeff Healey Band's first CD, See the Light.

Actually, not so cool after a while. One day, in particular, the movie's director wasn't happy with the shot for a bar scene in the film. Laura and Linda were bored out of their trees, sitting at the back of the studio with their parents as the scene was shot over and over. Linda thought she would lose her mind if they didn't move on to something else soon. Her chewing gum had lost its flavour long ago. She tipped back onto the rear legs of her chair, examining a dot on the ceiling that seemed more interesting than the hundredth take of the same blasted scene. But then just a microsecond before the director jumped up to shout "That's it!" as they finally nailed the scene, Linda tipped back that extra inch too much.

Crash!

The sound echoed through the studio like the aftershock of a dynamite blast. The scene was trashed. All heads turned as eyes bored into a sheepish Linda in a pile on the floor. How embarrassing! Not exactly the kind of impression she was hoping to make on Swayze.

In and around the band's busy schedule, early-morning radio and late-night television talk shows had to be squeezed in. The band appeared on all the hot late-night TV talk shows of the late 1980s: *Late Night with David Letterman*, *The Arsenio Hall Show*, and *The Tonight Show*.

Jeff, Laura, Patrick Swayze, and Linda on the set of *Road House* in California in 1988.

Did they get caught up in the glitz? The band members were trying to keep costs down, so they self-managed. For years they drove around in an old Volvo station wagon with no roof rack, finding a way to cram all their gear into its back end. They didn't do the limo thing unless someone else was picking up the tab, like the record company, or for special events or photo opportunities.

"A limo is not as convenient as you might think, anyway," says Rockman. "You have to crawl in and out. There's a lot to be said for a customized van."

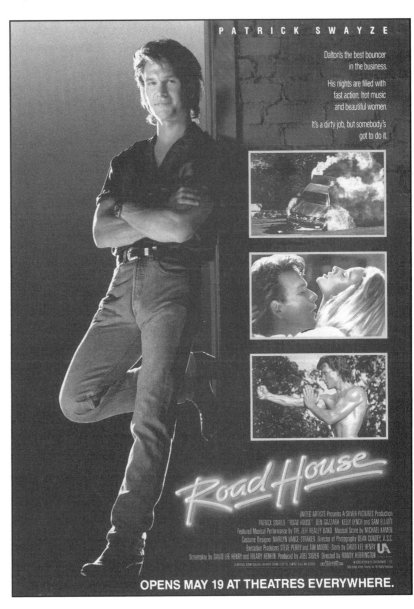

Poster for *Road House* starring Patrick Swayze. Jeff played Cody, the leader of the house band in the Double Deuce, the road house of the title.

The Jeff Healey Band: Awards and Stuff

1989

- Grammy Awards nomination Best Instrumental Rock Group
- Edison Award (Holland) Best Foreign Rock Group
- Juno Awards nomination Most Promising Male Vocalist (Jeff Healey)
- Billboard International Achievement Award
- COCA Award Entertainer of the Year
- International Rock Awards nomination Newcomer of the Year
- CASBY Award Best Male Vocalist (Jeff Healey)
- CASBY Award Album of the Year
- CASBY Award Single of the Year ("Angel Eyes")
- Toronto Music Awards Mayor's Award
- Toronto Music Award Best Toronto Guitarist (Jeff Healey)
- Toronto Music Award Best Toronto Group with International Acclaim
- Music Express Award Male Vocalist of the Year (Jeff Healey)
- Music Express Award Best Live Act of the Year
- Platinum sales award (Canada) for *See the Light*
- 2 x Platinum sales award (Canada) for *See the Light*
- Gold sales award (United States) for *See the Light*
- Gold sales award (Canada) for *Road House* soundtrack
- Juno Awards nomination Album of the Year (*See the Light*)
- Juno Award Canadian Entertainer of the Year
- World Music Award Bestselling Canadian Artist
- MuchMusic Canadian Music Video Award Best Group Video of the Year ("I Think I Love You Too Much")
- *Guitar Player* magazine readers' poll Best Blues Guitarist (Jeff Healey)
- *Guitar Player* magazine readers' poll Best New Talent (Jeff Healey)
- AMPEX Golden Reel Award Honouring the Recording of *See the Light*
- Platinum sales award (United States) for *See the Light*
- Silver Sales award (United Kingdom) for *See the Light*
- Platinum sales award (Canada) for *Hell to Pay*
- Gold sales award (United States) for *Hell to Pay*

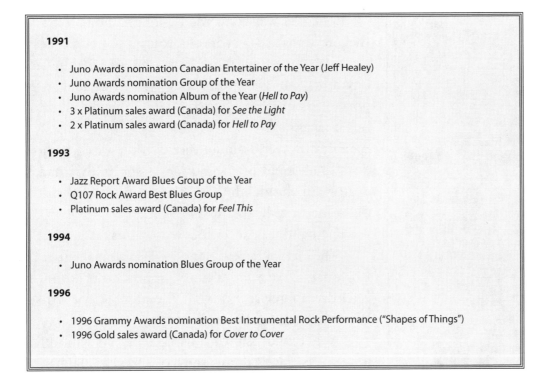

1991

- Juno Awards nomination Canadian Entertainer of the Year (Jeff Healey)
- Juno Awards nomination Group of the Year
- Juno Awards nomination Album of the Year (*Hell to Pay*)
- 3 x Platinum sales award (Canada) for *See the Light*
- 2 x Platinum sales award (Canada) for *Hell to Pay*

1993

- Jazz Report Award Blues Group of the Year
- Q107 Rock Award Best Blues Group
- Platinum sales award (Canada) for *Feel This*

1994

- Juno Awards nomination Blues Group of the Year

1996

- 1996 Grammy Awards nomination Best Instrumental Rock Performance ("Shapes of Things")
- 1996 Gold sales award (Canada) for *Cover to Cover*

But no matter how grounded you were, Hollywood was a whole different world. Scheduling life became a challenge; taking care of basics seemed impossible. Jet lag, stress, fast food, and round-the-clock stimulation created a pressure cooker: Jeff, Joe, and Tom were the meat being cooked. Speaking of meat, it didn't help Jeff's general well-being that he was a self-declared "carnivore." Even as an adult, it was still impossible to get him to eat his veggies.

"The only time he had vegetables," says Rockman, "was in soup or his Bloody Caesars." (A Bloody Caesar is an alcoholic drink made with clamato juice, sort of like V8, and garnished with celery.)

Advertisement for 1990 Juno Awards. The Jeff Healey Band was nominated for Album of the Year (*See the Light*) and Group of the Year. Jeff himself was nominated for Canadian Entertainer of the Year. He won.

Rockman was concerned enough about Jeff's health that he designed a workout routine especially for him. Because they often didn't have time to take the elevator down to the gym, Joe knew the routine had to be portable, something Jeff could do in his room, or on the bus if necessary.

But however draining the schedule was, and however distasteful some of the business aspects that had to be dealt with during the day, those two hours onstage at night made it all worthwhile.

The band was never focused on image.

"The Jeff Healey Band was beyond visual," says Rockman. "We were a music appreciators' band, not a celebrity appreciators' band. Besides, Jeff was riveting. We didn't need pink elephants."

"Angel Eyes" is probably the song Jeff is most famous for. It was the wedding song of the year. Thousands of couples danced their first dance as husband and wife to Jeff's soulful voice. Goodness knows how many young lovers had it as "their song." It's ironic that Jeff's hit tune was "Angel Eyes," considering he had lost his.

"Because Jeff was blind, he was an eye magnet," says Rockman. "It made him instantly recognizable."

But recognition is a double-edged sword. After striving for years to arrive there, to get to the point where people recognized you on the street, was it everything it was cracked up to be?

Jeff Healey

— Adrianna —

She walks on by, & you can't help but notice
Cause she catches your eye
Whenever she's around you feel you want
To touch her and to kiss her.
She's a girl who wants
Your memory, I've found.

Adriana, Tropicana.
Girl want you be mine.
Or are you just passing through
Just moving down the line.
Adrianna.

Her voice would melt
The coldest ice of winter
You never felt such warmth inside of
In all your dreams it never was you
quite like this
This girl it seems
Is just too good to be true.

Chorus.

She walks on past
And you can't help but follow,
But she goes too fast
And you get left alone.
With all your soul,
You hope again you'll see her.
Your only goal
Is to make that girl your own.
— Chorus —
And there's Adrianna.
And there's Adrianna! . . .
(Written by Jeff)

Jeff Mails Lyrics to Himself

To protect his original lyrics as a songwriter, Jeff would mail a sealed copy of the original written words to himself. This was a common practice in the industry. The postmark would prove he had written the song at that date if there was ever a dispute about who had authored the lyrics to a hit song. You had to save the sealed envelope, though, or it wouldn't work.

Lyrics for Jeff's song "Adrianna," the first Jeff Healey Band 44 rpm record.

"Yes, is the first answer," says Rockman. "We worked with some great people in the music industry, some as talented at what they do as Jeff was as an artist. Some who could play the music industry the way Jeff played the guitar. But the novelty wears off. It does become old after a while," he adds with a bittersweet laugh. "In the end, it can get in the way of what you're trying to do — create."

But Stephen and Rockman knew they "had to hit while the iron was hot," so the band did a massive amount of touring in the early years, booking two to three hundred shows annually, over and above the recording and promotional duties that came with the territory. That had to be tough.

Christmas 1992 card from The Jeff Healey Band: Joe Rockman, Jeff, and Tom Stephen.

"Of course, you get under each other's skin," says Rockman. "In my experience a necessary equation for a group's success is to live together, eat together, play together. That gets reflected in the music. It's closer than a marriage in some ways. You think each other's thoughts. But in those close quarters you're going to get on each other's nerves."

So how did the band stick together for so long? How did it work?

"Jeff was a genius," says Rockman "He was unique. I don't know if I can say that about myself. I'm a good collaborator because I have a collective mentality. That's what made it work. When the genius is screwing up, the sub-genius can tell him. Two geniuses can't work — ego gets in the way."

While Jeff was playing loud blues-based rock and roll, he was still at home listening to Louis Armstrong and other early jazz greats.

"So I think the lesson there," says Richard Flohil, "is whatever you do, do what you love to do, and at the same time, keep your ears wide open for other things."

Flohil was always amazed by Jeff's encyclopedic knowledge of early jazz, blues, rock and roll, and country — it didn't seem to matter what kind of music, Jeff knew it. He could move seamlessly from playing jazz one moment to "Hendrix-like psychedelic, out there music" the next, with no problem. It was just in his repertoire.

"His passion for music," says Flohil, "it didn't matter what kind of music, led him to what some people see as a schizophrenic musical career."

But what happens when your dreams come true and they aren't what you expected? When you find it isn't what you really want?

It didn't help that personal circumstances added pressure. There were times when it seemed as if everything was falling apart. Jeff's parents had sold their Etobicoke house on Bonnyview Drive in 1987 and moved to Lindsay, Ontario. Nobody understood it. Most of the family was still in Toronto; there was no connection to Lindsay. Even though Jeff was twenty-one and had moved away from home years before, he couldn't believe his parents had sold the family house.

The home had meant so much to him; he knew every nook and cranny. Jeff missed it, sometimes even returning to his old street to sit on the front step of the house. It didn't help that his mom was diagnosed with breast cancer almost immediately after the move. The family felt as if their world had turned upside down.

Laura remembers looking out the window in despair and thinking, *What's happening to us? Why? What's going on?*

Jeff got married in 1992. In 1994, four months after finding out he was expecting his first child, Jeff's mother succumbed to cancer at age fifty-five. Jeff was twenty-eight.

Family was always important to Jeff, so this was a huge blow. Yvonne Healey would never see her first grandchild, but Jeff was about to become a dad! That got him thinking about the hereditary nature of retinoblastoma. He felt compelled to learn about his birth family. Ironically, Jeff's birth mother had moved to Peterborough, Ontario, only minutes away from the new Healey home in Lindsay.

With lots of legwork and creative tracking by his first wife, Krista (who he married in 1992), Jeff was finally able to get contact information for his birth mother, only to have her hang up on him, saying, "Wrong number." Ouch. That had to sting.

She did call back a few days later, though, and let him know he had a full sibling, a sister, who she had kept (and who now had children of her own), but that she absolutely could not, would not, let her family know about Jeff. He tried to convince her that because of the seriousness of the disease, she had to find a way to tell her daughter about this cancer, to make sure she and her children were checked for the gene. At the time of his death, however, as far as Jeff knew, that had never happened.

"I was never looking for another mother or another sister," Jeff said, as quoted by Deborah A. Brennan in *Labours of Love*. "I was raised in a very close family and have so many friends. Mine is a rich life. But somewhere there is a lady that needs to know and her kids need to know. I've done what I can do."

Try This On

Using either Jeff or his birth mother's point of view, draft a letter to a birth sister, telling her about her brother and the retinoblastoma gene risk. How do you break the news?

With the birth of his baby girl, Rachel, Jeff began to resent his time away from home even more. The shine of stardom was starting to wear off. Near the end of his "rock star" years, "Jeff felt like a circus freak," according to his long-time friend Rob Quail. Those years were a dark period in Jeff's life.

"He felt isolated," Quail says, "his marriage [to Krista] broke down, his band relationship soured, he was locked into a record contract making music he didn't want to make anymore. He had no artistic control and he was travelling all the time … which he hated." Jeff and Krista were divorced in 1999.

"Stardom is no different than any extreme sports artist," says Rockman. "The music industry is an extreme sport. You're going to crash. How you pick yourself up to go to the next level, is the question."

Jeff with his daughter, Rachel, in January 2000.

15

THE JAZZ WIZARDS

By the year 2000, it was obvious to those who cared about him that Jeff's disillusionment with the world of rock music was a constant, bitter taste in his mouth. His dad thought he had worked his way to the top only to say, "Well, here I am. Why am I here?"

For Jeff, says Bud, "All that really counted was to be able to play the music and have people enjoy it. That's all that mattered."

Jeff looked back fondly on his Blue Direction days when he was still naive about the business side of the industry and played purely for the joy and discovery of it. Not content to sit back or follow the crowd, even after he had hit the "big time" and was famous for his unique brand of pop-blues-rock, he longed to return to his roots, to music he had always been passionate about — hot jazz.

It wasn't considered trendy. It wasn't likely to make him the big bucks. Everyone thought it was a crazy move. But Jeff believed in his music. He believed in the power of following his dreams.

Jeff Healey had come full circle, or so it seemed. Drawn to music out of his love for jazz and pulled into celebrity as a pop-blues artist, he found he had to answer the need to return to his roots to find his spirit again. Following his heart, Jeff committed to switching gears and pursuing his interest in early jazz and twentieth-century popular American music. In particular he loved 1920s and 1930s jazz.

His buddy Rob Quail laughs, remembering Jeff's views on "post-war jazz." "He believed it was all a conspiracy to dilute black music, to water down true great jazz. They moved away from the heart and loins, and it became intellectual."

Jeff hated that. That was why he stuck with early jazz; it was pure, untainted. But Rockman questions whether jazz can ever truly be what it was. "It was a product of its time," he says. "The mood of that time shaped it. We can only replicate it, but it will, at best, be a bright shadow because we never lived it."

As Jeff rekindled his passion and pure joy in music, his heart was opened in other ways. Both he and Cristie Hall, his second wife, were unsuspecting of what fate had in store when their paths first crossed on a warm summer night on July 11, 2001. Cristie was cajoled into heading out to karaoke night at Jeff Healey's bar for a friend's birthday. She wasn't in the mood. Being social was the last thing on her mind. But after some coaxing from her producer — she was working on her own CD at the time — she finally dragged her butt out of her one-bedroom apartment in East York and made her way down.

Getting into the spirit once she got to the club, Cristie submitted her name to take the stage. A long time seemed to pass, and when a few karaoke candidates took the mike for the second or third time, one of Cristie's gang decided to find out why she hadn't been called yet. It paid off. The lineup coordinator apologized and promised to put Cristie at the front of the line. But first he called up Jeff to sing. Not surprisingly, everyone hooted and hollered, anticipating the famous bar's namesake. After complaining that he was just on his way to the bathroom, Jeff began hamming it up, pretending to read the karaoke screen. He had the audience in the palm of his hand before he even started to sing.

Cristie was thrilled until about halfway through his song when panic kicked in as it suddenly occurred to her. *Oh, my God! I'm going to have to get up and sing after him?*

Sure enough, as Jeff finished the last melancholy notes of his tune to raucous applause, Cristie's name was called. She went onstage and peered out over the expectant audience. "Now how am I supposed to follow *that*?" she asked the crowd.

Everyone laughed, taking the edge off her nerves and easing her into a haunting version of Sarah McLachlan's "Angel." Her voice caught Jeff's attention. The washroom could wait. He sought Cristie out as she got off the stage, and the rest, as they say, is history. They connected. At first it was merely a business relationship, with Jeff giving advice about Cristie's singing career, but after a couple of months of weekly get-togethers and late-night chat sessions, they both acknowledged that this was something more, something different.

"We changed each other's lives," says Cristie. "I saw something different. I saw something else. We approached each other differently than we had with anyone else, and that's how it clicked."

And so one year later Jeff proposed in Wiarton, Ontario, offering up a ring that three of Cristie's girlfriends helped pick out. The ecstatic couple married on July 18, 2003, almost a year to the day he proposed. Cristie knew her dad approved. Jeff was the only person who could out-eat her father when it came to turkey and mashed potatoes, but ever the veggie-hater, he always declined Brussels sprouts, a family staple. One night at her parents' place for dinner, Jeff scooped a huge heap of mashed potatoes into his mouth, and Cristie thought he was going to pop an eye.

"Oh, Jeff must have found that Brussels sprout I slipped into his potatoes," her father said calmly.

"That's when I knew my dad loved Jeff," Cristie says.

It seems Jeff was destined to have people who cared about him try to sneak veggies into his spuds.

Did Cristie pursue her singing career?

"I didn't," she says. "I finished my CD, I went on the road with Jeff to Brazil, I sang with the band a few times, but I opted not to pursue it. I got to look at 'on the road' life and started thinking, *What do I want? What's more important to me?* It was more important to me to have a family."

And so little Derek Healey was born on March 7, 2005. Cristie didn't want to know the sex in advance, but Jeff had begged her.

"I promise I'll keep it a secret," he said. "Even from you. I need to know."

As a child, he had always gotten along better with girls; boys were more likely to pick on him. The idea of having a boy made Jeff nervous.

What am I going to teach a boy? he thought. *How am I going to do this?*

But all doubts disappeared when he met Derek. And the feeling seemed to be mutual. All those conversations with Cristie's belly during the pregnancy, and the personalized soundtracks Jeff had prepared as bedtime music, paid off. In a crowded delivery room Derek's head swivelled to find Jeff when he spoke. Within minutes of being born, baby Derek immediately knew the voice that had captivated millions around the world.

Jeff's worries about how he was going "to do it" were for nothing. Cristie often overheard him with Derek in the next room as they played.

"How did I ever live my life without you?" he would whisper before letting Derek tackle him to the floor.

Did You Know?

The last song Jeff Healey ever sang at a public performance was one of his favourite tunes, "Stardust," from the *Among Friends* CD.

While the prospect of being a father had terrified Jeff initially, he loved it. A big kid at heart himself, he loved being the "silly daddy." When he talked about either of his children, whether his "Rachie" or Derek, he glowed, a perma-grin lighting his face.

Jeff's renewed passion for his music deepened his capacity to love again. His profound love for his family also brought greater depth to his new-old jazz. He produced three jazz CDs and travelled worldwide both as a solo performer and as Jeff Healey and the Jazz Wizards. Jeff's dad believes that of all his son's musical accomplishments, Jeff was probably most proud of those three jazz CDs. They represented his passion and his first love.

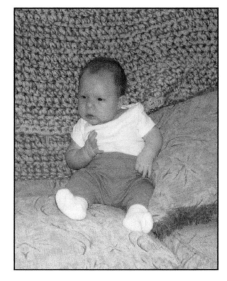

Jeff's son, Derek, born on March 7, 2005.

Rob Quail agrees. He believes that Jeff would want his legacy to be helping to keep that music alive. Jeff felt it was the "noblest of human creations." He wanted the music archived and was in the process of cataloguing his massive 78 rpm album collection. He only got as far as *M*, but he became respected around the world for bringing great jazz music back to life.

While Cristie would agree that most people think Jeff's legacy should be his music, she believes it is more about how Jeff conducted his life. "It's the determination, the strength. He never let anybody tell him you're not capable. He was picked on because he was different. He had insecurities just like any other kid, but he had a goal and he never stopped."

Again putting his money where his mouth was, in a true labour of love, Jeff produced a three-CD set of every single track his hero, Louis Armstrong, had played with a group led by Fletcher Henderson. Nobody had ever collected them together in one place.

Jeff Healey's CDs

- **1988**: *See the Light*
- **1989**: *Road House Soundtrack*
- **1990**: *Hell to Pay*
- **1992**: *Feel This*
- **1995**: *Cover to Cover*
- **2000**: *Get Me Some*
- **2002**: *Among Friends*
- **2003**: *Live at Healey's*
- **2004**: *Adventures in Jazzland*
- **2005**: *The Jeff Healey Band Live at Montreux 1999*
- **2006**: *It's Tight Like That*
- **2008**: *Mess of Blues*
- **2009**: *Songs from the Road*

Poster for Jeff's *Adventures in Jazzland* CD.

"Of forty-eight tracks, Jeff was only missing one, which appeared to have vanished off the face of the Earth," says Richard Flohil. "It was a huge discovery for me. I'm always grateful to Jeff for that."

Jeff subscribed to a theory his publicist touted. When a young musician said, "Hey, man, you've got to discover new music," he would say, "No, discover old music — it'll be new to you."

Jeff Healey was universally respected in the music industry. Artists who had played with him had nothing but praise for his musical abilities, passion, and dedication, but equally important, for his grace as a person. Jeff never lost sight of where he had come from. He was down-to-earth and real.

Flohil recalls the live album Jeff did with Chris Barber, a famous Dixieland jazz band trombonist hailing from England. "It opens with a tune called 'Bugle Call Rag' and has a little sort of fanfare, and then the band comes in. Jeff blows two clams in the intro. I say, 'Jeff, for crying out loud, can't you go in the studio and fix that?' He says, 'No, that's the way it was.' And it stayed."

Other Musicians Talk About Jeff

Randy Bachman: "Jeff and I somehow felt a brotherhood with each other. Every time we'd meet, it would be a hug and a handshake of true affection. I travelled with him, dined with him, performed with him, and recorded with him. Every moment was special. I will never forget them. Jeff was one of the best guitar players in the entire world. He could get onstage with the greatest and make them sweat. He always 'stole the show' from whomever he performed with. He had that magic to dazzle everyone. I miss him and our time together."

David Wilcox: "The thing I would most comment on is his accessibility as a person. He made you right at home. He was down-to-earth, gracious, aware and humble, for all his brilliance. I hate to say I'm competitive, but when Jeff was playing, let's face it, he made you play your best … he spurred you on. If Jeff Healey was playing, you wanted to do your best."

Colin James: "There have been players that played upside down and backward — Jimi Hendrix, Albert King. That's unorthodox enough. And then Jeff made that look trite. Jeff was an amazing talent. A one-of-a-kind player who challenged the norms to become one of the best in the world in his genre. If you ever wondered if someone was born to be a musician, I think that answer is in the life of Jeff Healey."

Joe Rockman: "Jeff had a direct tap into the Muse. He would absorb musical ideas through osmosis, then draw upon his encyclopedic knowledge to create sounds that would consistently surprise and move you. In the thousands of shows we played, I was never bored. The depth and execution — there was an urgency in his guitar playing, something unique. I would use the word *prodigy*. Jeff downplayed it, but his technique gave him different ways of phrasing his music. It set him apart."

Did You Know?

When Richard Flohil says Jeff blew two "clams," he isn't talking about seafood. A *clam* is slang for a bad note.

16

IT'S OKAY
TO BE BLIND

Jeff Healey never saw himself as overcoming adversity, never felt short-changed. You played the hand you were dealt. Similarly, Laura and Linda never thought of Jeff as blind or different. They played baseball, hockey, cards, games; they fished, swam, rode bikes; they laughed, cried, fought, argued; they did everything sighted siblings would do together. They might have found different ways to do some of those things, whether putting stones in the baseball so Jeff could hear, scrunching old tins as hockey pucks so they would rattle across the ice, or using Braille card decks.

Some people assume that blindness is somehow a lesser experience of life. But is it? Look at Jeff's passion for music, his knowledge, his skill, his appreciation of life. Was his experience diminished by his blindness? Was it possible it might have been enhanced?

"Once you get past the emotions, blindness is purely technical," says Jim Sanders, former director of the Canadian National Institute for the Blind. "Blindness is more of an occasional nuisance, like being six foot six. You have to learn to duck through a door once in a while."

How can we understand, get a taste of what it must be like? Closing your eyes might let you simulate the physical act of being blind, but really, blindness is about the skills you need to learn.

"Eighty to ninety percent of what we learn, know, and are able to do is through light images coming into our eyes," says Sanders. "When that's no longer possible, we learn through our other senses — touch, hearing, smell, and taste."

Salt and Pepper

Question: Without your eyesight, consider how you would tell the difference between salt and pepper.

Answer: Pepper is lighter than salt, so lift the shakers and see if you can tell. If that doesn't work, sprinkle a bit on your hand and smell. If that doesn't work, put a bit on your tongue and taste. Of course, if you sneeze, it's probably pepper!

Sanders speaks from experience. He wasn't born blind. He remembers what it is to be able to see, to read print if he held the book close to his nose. When you are born blind, what you do is natural. By contrast, when you lose your sight later in life, as he did, you grieve the loss at first. The challenge is to learn the skills you need to function efficiently, and know that once you do, it will be okay.

One of the most important messages to instill in blind children, Sanders believes, is that it's okay to be blind. You don't have to apologize, feel awkward, or despair. "The only difference between blind and sighted people is the manner in which they send and receive some types of information," he says.

Hmm. Read that a few times. Say it out loud. What does he mean? Blind people read, write, and communicate as do sighted people. How they do it might be different, that's all, whether through Braille, a note-taker, or any of the other assisting technologies.

We all do and experience the same things in life, but in varying ways. Sighted people watch the sunrise, while blind people feel its warmth spread as the sun peeks over the horizon and rises into the morning sky. Sighted people avoid obstacles, while blind people seek them out, needing them to orientate themselves to determine where a curb, a chair, or some other object is.

Sanders isn't the only one with a dream to share that it's okay to be blind. Newfoundland-born singer songwriter Terry Kelly travels the world, delivering his message through song and motivational speeches.

Imagine a world where we don't judge others based on appearance or perceived disabilities, where we acknowledge people and their worth first, where it is no big deal to be blind or different. Kelly's newest CD speaks to this theme. The recording is the first commercially produced music CD in the world with Braille liner notes. "The Power of the Dream," the title track, is a powerful song about transforming what it means to be blind by changing attitudes.

"I have always been a dreamer," says Kelly. "I will always be a dreamer. I have discovered that the power of the dream gives hope, strength, courage, empowerment, and brings about profound transformation in individuals and groups of people if one simple rule is followed — honour the dream by taking action."

Nobody can accuse Kelly of not practising what he preaches. Like Jeff Healey, Kelly was diagnosed with retinoblastoma as an infant, losing first one, then both eyes to the disease. As a child, he was sent from his family to Halifax School for the Blind, a residential school much like W. Ross Macdonald. Kelly learned

Try This On

Try a little experiment to see how much you rely on your sight to get around. Consider as a class project, or at home with supervision, pairing up and having each partner take turns blindfolded. Make sure you can't see around the edges and that no light gets in. Enlist your partner as a "sighted guide" and/or use a white cane. The blindfolded partner gets a handful of change to keep in his or her pocket. Then head out to a local store you know well to buy your favourite chocolate bar (or to the playground to play on your favourite piece of equipment—modify the exercise as necessary).

Even though you think you know the way there, and your way around the store (or playground), you might be surprised at how easily you get turned around, how disoriented you will become. Your depth perception (awareness of how close/far things are from you) will be way off-kilter, which in turn will affect your balance and coordination. You might even find that you confuse left versus right, up versus down.

to play the accordion, clarinet, guitar, and piano. He has been nominated for Juno and Canadian Country Music Awards and has won six East Coast Music Awards, one in every category in which he was nominated that year. He has six full-length recordings to his credit and gives motivational speeches around the world. As an athlete, Terry was a double silver medallist at the 1979 Canadian Track Championships, competed in the 1980 Paralympics, ran the mile in under five minutes, and carried the Olympic Torch in the 1988 Winter Olympics in Calgary. Who says blindness slows you down?

Kelly and Healey share more than common medical histories. Jeff believed that you could achieve whatever you put your mind to if you kept a positive attitude and "just did it." So does Kelly.

"As with anything in life," Jim Sanders echoes, "more than your skills, eighty percent of your successes will depend on your attitude."

Jeff had plenty of that. He is universally described by those who knew him as an optimist, someone with a great attitude and real sense of humour about his blindness. He was never embarrassed, choosing instead to diminish other people's awkwardness and uncertainty through jokes.

Richard Flohil remembers one meeting with Jeff, after his own wedding. Flohil didn't even know Jeff had been at his wedding until he saw him in a photo with Sylvia Tyson and Raffi.

What an unlikely trio! Flohil thought.

A few weeks later, at a big launch party for one of Jeff's records, Flohil apologized. "Jeff, I'm sorry I didn't see you at our wedding."

Without missing a beat, Jeff answered. "I didn't see you, either."

How do you maintain a positive attitude when you first face blindness? Having a positive role model can help a great deal. Take Jim Sanders as an example. Sure, his parents were scared when told at his birth he would lose his sight by the age of six. But then they met the early-intervention specialist sent to counsel them, a young, highly functioning, intelligent, blind man with a family of his own. Jim's mother was immediately put at ease. She couldn't remember much of what he had told them, but when he left, she said, "Everything's going to be okay." Having a positive role model gave her peace of mind, strength to deal with challenges as they arose, provided her with the positive attitude she needed to find the perspective to succeed. In fact, she was so reassured that she and her husband had nine more kids!

Jeff's parents had a similar experience. "We wanted so much for him to live and grow," says Bud Healey, "yet were so afraid he wouldn't have the chance."

CNIB early-intervention specialist Doris Weaver came out to see Jeff's parents when the future guitarist was a toddler. "Don't treat him as if he's handicapped," Weaver warned. "Make sure you treat him like any ordinary kid." Her other caution was to make sure they didn't allow Jeff to rock (and no, she didn't mean rock and roll). "It's a bad habit," she told them.

Little did they know that Jeff would give new meaning to the term *rock*.

In the same way that these early-intervention specialists gave hope for normalcy to the Healeys and Sanders, Jeff became an inspiration for blind people and their families. Jim Sanders sees this as one of Jeff's greatest contributions. "Jeff recognized and took

---

"The Power of the Dream"

Excerpted from the song by Terry Kelly. Released in March 2002. Gun Records, Inc.

Look, see there, movement
Everywhere improvement
150 million tongues, one clear voice!
From the land down under
A song the sound of thunder
Singing the dream to opening ears
All over the world!

There's a buzz in the air
And the people from far and near
Have made a choice; the choice is clear!

Chorus

Changing what it means to be blind
Step by step one day at a time
Still much to do but it shall be
That the sighted eyes of the world
Will be able to see
And there will be changes
The power of the dream
Due diligence by you and me
Changing what it means to be blind

Rock and Roll

Have you ever noticed that many blind people rock themselves? Ray Charles and Stevie Wonder were both known for it. Some say the rocking motion gives them a sense of space, of where they are, but it's more generally believed that it's just a source of stimulation. Sighted people are constantly barraged with visual stimulation without even being aware of it. For blind people the movement is a means of self-stimulation. Try to sit with your eyes closed for as long as you can. After a few minutes, you will probably start to move … to rock. Perhaps just your head at first, but you *will* feel the need to move — to get some stimulation.

very seriously his obligation to represent normalcy. He was a great example of a highly functioning, effective blind person, the perfect role model."

As it turned out, Bud and Yvonne Healey also learned from their son. "Jeff inspired us," Bud says, as quoted by A Life Worth Living's Judy Robinet. "He used all of his senses to find his way. He had an uncanny ability to remember people and places. His curiosity and motivation to learn gave us the strength and will to keep going."

Jeff made sure he acquired whatever skills he needed to fully participate and experience life. "He was very determined," says Laura, Jeff's sister. "Just because he couldn't see didn't mean he had to stop doing things he wanted to in life. Everyone has setbacks. Jeff just never let anything stop him."

He was fiercely independent and insisted on doing everything himself. Jeff refused to have a seeing-eye dog. He was naturally reluctant due to his fear of larger dogs, but mostly he just didn't want to be dependent on anyone or anything.

"Nope, I'm doing it on my own," he would say.

Jeff took the bus and subway alone from a young age despite a few mishaps. With dogged determination he even lugged his guitar and amplifier around single-handed. Jeff got into the habit of keeping any incidents to himself. He especially avoided telling his mother, partly because he knew she would worry, but really because he didn't want to give his parents any excuse to curtail his freedom.

One evening, busy sorting the dirty clothes, Yvonne pulled Jeff's new white jeans out of his laundry hamper. They weren't white anymore. When she saw the marks, she stopped and shook her head, then called Bud in to check it out.

"Look at this mess," she said. "What could he possibly be doing to get them this dirty?"

Bud's heart jumped. He had just done a routine fire tour of the subway two days earlier. He recognized the soot from the subway's tunnels. This couldn't be good. He didn't dare say anything to Yvonne. Better she think Jeff didn't bother to take care of his clothes than the frightening alternative running through his head. The worried dad immediately went upstairs to confront Jeff one-on-one until he finally confessed.

Jeff had been playing a gig in downtown Toronto and was catching the last subway train home for the night. As usual he waited at the top end of the platform so he could enter the first car. But the subway stopped short that night, and a tired Jeff hadn't sensed it. When he heard the train squeal to a stop, echoing through the nearly deserted platform, Jeff stepped forward, expecting to step through an open doorway into the train. Instead he stepped into open space and fell onto the tracks. Now that was a rude awakening after a long night. Luckily, the subway operator saw what had happened, reacted immediately, and shut down the power on the track. Five hundred and fifty volts were running through those rails!

A few weeks later Bud was on another fire tour of the subway and was talking to an inspector about strange things that occurred on the job. The inspector began to tell him about a blind boy who had fallen onto the tracks a few weeks earlier.

Guide Dogs

According to orientation and mobility specialist Scott Johnston, as a general rule, you must be eighteen years old to qualify for a guide dog. First, you need to develop good skills with a white cane. You also require well-developed orientation skills and a higher level of independence.

Contrary to popular belief, the guide dog doesn't take you where you want to go. You need to direct the dog with appropriate commands, i.e., "forward," "find the stairs."

"It's actually easier to get lost with guide dogs," says Johnston. "You're more likely to miss important tactile information, like feeling the grass shoulder with the cane."

Guide dogs aren't for everyone. "If you don't already have good spatial awareness, a guide dog won't work," says Johnston.

You also have to be able to take care of the dog and keep the animal disciplined so that it doesn't lose its skills. The most common dog breeds used for the Canine Vision Program are Labrador retrievers, standard poodles, and golden retrievers.

"That's my boy," Bud said.

The inspector happened to be the same guy who had driven Jeff home that night. Jeff had refused to go to the hospital and had only grudgingly agreed to let the night inspector drive him home after much convincing. Talk about a small-world story!

Audible Intersections

Ever wonder how the sound signals at street intersections work? The sounds seem to blast out from everywhere. How do the visually impaired know which direction is safe? If you listen closely, you will notice that there are two distinct sounds — a cuckoo and a chirping. The cuckoo means it is safe to travel north and south. The chirping means it is okay to proceed east and west. But not all intersections are created equal. Of those that have audible signals, some aren't automatic. You need to push a button to activate the signals. The problem, though, is that not all intersections have locator sounds for the button that needs to be pushed! How is a blind person supposed to find the button? If you can't push the button to activate the audible signal, it doesn't really provide much assistance.

As another step to his self-sufficiency, Jeff learned to type, even before much of today's assistive communication technology had come into being.

Can you type? Do you use the one-fingered seek-and-peck method or all your fingers? Don't forget that Jeff was born in the 1960s before computers were considered a must-have commodity. He learned on a traditional typewriter. Typewriters don't have delete keys or backspace buttons that magically erase your last mistake. The Healeys left a small typewriter by the phone so that Jeff could type out messages when someone called.

By all accounts, Jeff was a "brilliant typist." Richard Flohil recalls Jeff typing the sleeve notes for the live Chris Barber joint CD venture on a machine he had never used before. "He was typing away like crazy. At one point I leaned over to ask something, and he said, 'Don't interrupt me. Unlike you, I can't see where I was if I pause.' When he was done, he sent it over to my computer. I looked it over and found only one typing error — in a six-hundred-word piece!"

Did Jeff mind being blind?

He didn't want attention drawn to his blindness or his unusual technique. He got bored talking about it and didn't want it to become the focus. The music was the important thing. And Jeff didn't view his blindness as impacting on his music. When journalists suggested that Jeff's style of playing was like reading Braille, reading the guitar through touch and feel, Jeff balked. "It's just the way I play, man." When people suggested that his musical intuition was sharpened because of the loss of his sight, Jeff would merely shrug.

"He wasn't less skilled because he was blind," says Jim Sanders. "He probably wasn't more skilled because of it. It didn't impact on him."

Jeff would agree. Bandmate Joe Rockman thought there was more to it. "His ears didn't hear more because he was blind. But his brain did. But Jeff would dispute that."

Blind People Have Better Hearing — Fact or Myth?

Here's what Peter Engel and Merrit Malloy, in *Old Wives' Tales: The Truth About Everyday Myths*, have to say about blind people having better hearing: "According to a study done by Seymour Axelrod, Ph.D., the blind are much better at the task of 'sound relocation' because they are much more practiced at it. That is to say that blind people, out of necessity, develop that acquired skill. They can't actually *hear* better, but they can listen better. The input from their ears is processed in a more 'focused' way."

Sure, being blind had setbacks on tour. Jeff couldn't see the sights for one thing. Bandmate Joe Rockman would take the time to describe the visuals, to try to put into words the experience of the first sight of the ocean or mountains. The challenge of an ever-changing environment could be tricky sometimes. Knowing where everything belongs and keeping everything in place are important survival techniques for a blind person. But Jeff fared well in that department, using what he called "sonic locating." On first meeting Jeff, Rockman noticed that the guitarist often snapped his fingers. For a while he thought Jeff was keeping the beat to some internal song, but later he discovered that Jeff was looking for the reflections of the snap to locate couches or other objects.

Jeff even adapted relatively easily to the acoustic problem onstage. The cacophony onstage can be disorienting for any artist. Jeff didn't want to use new wireless earphone technology to combat the problem. He didn't want his ears plugged by anything that would interfere with his "sonic location." But somehow he always managed. He seemed to have perfect spatial awareness onstage, almost always finding his way easily back to his chair.

In his life Jeff probably had only one serious complaint about his blindness. "The only thing that bothered Jeff about not being able to see was that he couldn't see his children," says Bud Healey.

Everyone agrees that of all his lifetime achievements, Jeff was probably the most proud of his children. He would often say, "I've got the best kids in the whole world."

When Jeff died, his daughter, Rachel, was thirteen years old, his son, Derek, only three. Looking at Derek is like seeing a "mini-Jeff," a spitting image. Beyond his good looks, there is speculation that young Derek might have more in common with his dad. After Jeff's funeral service, a bunch of his musician friends jumped when the sound of drums startled them out of their reminiscing. All heads turned to the drums. At first they couldn't see anyone. Was a ghost beating out its compelling rhythm? But then they spotted a familiar tuft of blond hair and recognized little Derek playing. Not just whacking the skins as you would expect a little kid to do, but really playing — making music. Self-taught at three years old … sound familiar?

Unfortunately, that wasn't the only thing Derek inherited from his dad. He was diagnosed early with the retinoblastoma gene. At thirty-two weeks pregnant Cristie Healey had an amniocentesis done to test Derek's DNA. It confirmed that her son had the gene mutation.

How did Jeff and Cristie react?

"I was mortified," says Cristie. "Devastated. But Jeff even more so. He put a lot of undue guilt on himself. He was absolutely crushed."

But research and technology have come a long way since Jeff was an infant. Derek had aggressive tumours growing for his first year and a half, but with a few surgeries already behind him, he still has his eyesight and his prognosis looks good. Keep your fingers crossed for him.

Jeff wanted to help other children, assist in finding a cure for retinoblastoma, and make a difference in the lives of blind children. He did a lot of charity work and was a key element in fundraising efforts on behalf of the CNIB, Toronto's Hospital for Sick Children, and the Daisy's Eye Cancer Fund. As usual he always brought his disarming sense of humour to any event. Once, he grabbed the camera from a TV crew and started filming. While playing golf at a charity fundraiser on another occasion, he drove the ball, shielded his eyes, and peered out over the fairway. "Did anyone see where the ball went?" he quipped.

Asked whether flash photography would bother him, Jeff smiled and pointed out, "I have no eyes. I don't have a visual impairment ... I have no eyes."

Jeff was also a big advocate for literacy. Once he learned Braille, both regular and music, there was no stopping him. His sisters remember him reading all the time, but asked what Jeff's favourite books were, Laura and Linda laugh. "How would we know what

Daisy's Eye Cancer Fund

Founded in 2004, the International Retinoblastoma Daisy Fund (IRDF) is named after Daisy Lloyd, a child from the United Kingdom diagnosed with a rare type of eye cancer. Daisy required specialized treatment at the Hospital for Sick Children in Toronto that was unavailable at home. Her parents established the Daisy Fund to raise money to cover costs when she travelled from the United Kingdom to Canada. Now the fund helps children around the world get access to the treatment they need to combat retinoblastoma.

Check out *www.daisyseyecancerfund.ca*.

Jeff Healey devoted a lot of his time to doing benefits for organizations such as Daisy's Eye Cancer Fund and Toronto's Hospital for Sick Children. On May 3, 2008, a couple of months after Jeff's death, many of his musical friends gathered to stage *A Celebration* at Toronto's Sound Academy, with proceeds going to two of Jeff's favourite charities.

113

In support of

The Canadian
National
CNIB Institute
for the Blind
Ontario Division

the 6th annual

Jeff Healey
Golf Classic
Monday, August 23, 1999

Dinner Sponsored by **AMJ CAMPBELL VAN LINES**

Beginning in the early 1990s, Jeff lent his time and energy to the Jeff Healey Golf Classic in support of the Canadian National Institute for the Blind.

he was reading?" Laura asks. "It was in Braille. But he always had a book on the go."

Jeff worked to promote Braille as a necessary skill, the equivalent of reading print for sighted kids. Jim Sanders agrees. In fact, Jim believes Braille is actually more efficient than print. Braille is simpler to learn than regular alphabet symbols. People can read Braille at four hundred words per minute, which is much faster than people can talk.

New technology helps level the playing field between blind and sighted people, but access to technology is one key area that still needs work to help the equalization. Technology has developed in great leaps forward, but unless blind people can access the technology they need, regardless of income level, there will always be an inequity. The challenge remains to ensure universal access.

"It shouldn't be thought of as charity," Jim Sanders comments, "but as a return on investment. What blind people can contribute if given the tools and skills necessary is tremendous."

Jeff Healey is a classic example of that.

Braille

Have you ever noticed raised dots on elevator buttons, menus, or bank machine pads? Would you know how to read them?

Braille, named after its inventor Louis Braille, employs a system of small raised dots "read" by a person's fingertips. The dots can be understood as words, numbers, or music. On the flip side, Braille can be used to take notes by punching out the dots with a pointed instrument. The readable raised dots appear on the other side of the paper.

How does Braille work? The system is simple. It is based on a "Braille cell," which consists of six dots numbered in a specific order. Each dot or combination of dots stands for a letter of the alphabet. Numbers and punctuation signs are also represented in Braille, with numbers indicated by a sign using dots 3, 4, 5, and 6. Capital letters are identified by a dot 6 just before the letter.

Much as sighted people learn the alphabet as a kid, blind people devote considerable time and practice to master Braille. But it is a critical skill to learn. Braille is to the blind person what the printed word is to the sighted. Even with new technology like voice-activated software, it is still important for blind children to learn Braille. Do you think education boards would announce that reading is being taken out of the curriculum, no longer required because we have voice technology and computers that can read for us? Not likely.

As the CNIB points out on its website (*www.cnib.ca*), "All children need to be literate — to read, write, and count — in order to enjoy intellectual freedom, personal security, and equal opportunities when they grow up."

Louis Braille

January 4, 2009, was the two hundredth anniversary of the birth of Louis Braille, the man responsible for developing the method used worldwide as the standard form of reading and writing by people who are blind or living with vision loss.

In 1812 three-year-old Louis was playing in his father's shoemaking shop in a small town near Paris when he accidentally punctured his eye with an awl (a sharp tool used to punch holes in leather). Health care and research weren't as advanced as today, so infection set in and young Louis eventually went blind in both eyes.

But he was smart and determined. At ten years old he earned a scholarship to the Royal Institution for Blind Youth in Paris. That's where Louis was first introduced to the idea of a coded system of raised letters. Charles Barbier de la Serre, a French army captain, had developed a system intended for the army, for soldiers to communicate silently at night. The army rejected the idea, but Barbier pursued it for possible use by blind people.

Barbier's system was too complicated, but Braille saw the potential. A tactile system that could be employed for reading and writing could be a valuable tool. He experimented, trying to find a simplified version, until in 1829, at only twenty years old, he came up with the Braille system used today.

Eight Things You Should Know About Being Blind

These are the top things you should know about being blind, including pet peeves about the things sighted people say or do that tick off the visually impaired (as presented by a group of blind or visually impaired teens attending an independent living skills course through the CNIB).

- Don't hold your fingers up in front of my face and ask how many fingers you're holding up. It's rude and it drives us crazy.
- Don't talk about me in the third person as if I'm invisible.
- Blind people aren't deaf or dim-witted. You don't need to yell or talk down to me.
- Don't be afraid to come up and talk to me. Just come up and say "Hi." Don't be uncomfortable around me just because I'm blind. We can sense your discomfort. It's almost a feeling in the air.
- Let me know when you walk away. I hate finding out that I'm left talking to air.
- Let me know that you're talking to me. If I don't answer, I'm not being rude. I probably don't know you're talking to me. Come close and address me directly.
- Don't feel sorry for me. Don't pity me.
- Don't patronize me.

World Braille Day

Several readers have asked us about World Braille Day in Canada. January 4, Louis Braille's birthday, is dedicated to raising awareness of the importance of braille. The ability to read and write braille opens the door to literacy for those unable to read print. Attending the celebrations at Healey's in Toronto on January 4, 2002, are, left to right, CNIB President and CEO Jim Sanders, musician and club owner Jeff Healey, the Honourable Senator Joyce Fairbairn, and musician Terry Kelly.

CNIB vision   Spring 2002

Six Advantages of Being Blind

Are there advantages to being blind? You bet, according to a group of visually impaired and/or blind teens. Here's what they had to say:

- We don't judge people by how they look.
- We tend to appreciate life more. We enjoy parts of life that sighted people take for granted.
- We can read in the dark.
- We can still function in a blackout.
- We focus on the things we can do.
- We get discounts on travel and transit.

17

WHO SAYS YOU CAN'T DRIVE BLIND?

Do you think Jeff Healey could drive? The obvious answer would be no.

But then, as Jeff's wife, Cristie, says, "Kids were always intrigued and amazed at what Jeff could do and what he couldn't do. They see it in a way adults don't."

So maybe it won't surprise you to hear that Jeff did drive … at least a few times.

In the Snow

With typically cold Canadian winters, it's no wonder Jeff's mom worried about his glass eyes getting cold, especially when Jeff went snowmobiling. No, you didn't read that wrong — Jeff went snowmobiling as a kid. When winter hit and the snow lay thick on the ground, Jeff's dad loaded up the family snowmobile and off they went to the Wiltons' farm where Jeff and the Wilton kids tore around the property, cutting tracks in the fresh snow. Sometimes Jeff would have another kid on the back of his sled to guide him, sometimes not.

But to make sure Jeff's eyes didn't get cold, his mother wrapped a scarf, mummy-style, around his entire face. That couldn't have been too comfortable. Remember how nasty it feels when your scarf gets soggy from your hot breath if it covers your mouth on a cold winter day? Poor Jeff! Imagine that soggy scarf tight over your whole face. It must have been a bit nerve-racking for the Wilton boys, too. Imagine a faceless boy on a snowmobile bearing down on you out of white-on-white snowdrifts.

Venturing off the property, Jeff still drove, but Uncle Lloyd had to sit behind him and direct. Occasionally, though, Uncle Lloyd got his right and left mixed up.

"Go left, Jeff," he would say with a vague point to the right.

Jeff would stop the sled dead in its tracks. "Which is it, Uncle Lloyd? Left or right?"

It was a good thing Jeff understood Uncle Lloyd's inconsistent directions, or who knows what trouble they might have ended up in?

Land Ahoy

Jeff must have gotten a taste for driving. In later years he was even known to grab the Jeep from the *Road House* set and career around the studio with a little help from his friends.

Once bitten, he decided he just had to drive The Jeff Healey Band tour bus. Not one to let a little thing like lack of sight stand in his way, Jeff had the driver find a big, empty parking lot, took a brief lesson, and off he went, veering the forty-five-foot-long bus around the lot, head thrown back, whooping with delight into the night.

With a Jeep and tour bus under his belt, it was only a small step to commandeer the golf cart and drive resigned bandmate Joe Rockman around the course during fundraising golf tournaments.

Anchors Away

Conquering snow and concrete, Jeff turned his attention to water next. On tour with The Jeff Healey Band he decided to try his hand serving as captain. The group had rented a few ski boats from a high-end resort. With the California sun beating down on them, Joe Rockman took the lead, making sure to break a traffic-free path around the huge lake. Jeff brought up the rear of their mini-convoy, manning the controls of his own watercraft. How did he know where to go? He followed the sound of the wake from Joe's boat. Would you trust your senses enough to drive a speedboat blindfolded, with only the sound of the boat in front of you to navigate by? No doubt a terrified rental operator looked on, mouth wide open, as his pricey investment blasted by with a blind man at the helm.

It's a Bird ... It's a Plane ...

Always one for a dare, Jeff wanted to try everything. With land and water under his belt, the skies were next. Do musicians gravitate to flying? Maybe because playing an instrument involves multi-tasking, some say piloting comes naturally to musicians. Jeff was no exception. Playing a gig in western Canada, Jeff and bandmate Joe Rockman were approached by a bush pilot out of Calgary who offered a ride through the Rocky Mountains in a Cessna.

Jeff jumped at the chance. He loved roller coasters, and this was sure to be a good ride. Sure enough, as soon as the plane hit cruising altitude, the pilot handed over the controls to let Jeff co-pilot the aircraft. He took to it like a pro with an instinctive feel for riding the currents.

At least nobody had to worry about Jeff getting lost. He amazed people with his keen, unerring sense of direction. You could ask Jeff how to get just about anywhere in Toronto, or somewhere he had visited, and he would give step-by-step directions for the most direct route there, leaving people wondering, *How did he do that?*

18

FINAL CURTAIN CALL

At thirty-nine years old, perhaps when everyone had stopped worrying about the chance of a cancer recurrence, when they thought they were home-free, Jeff was diagnosed with a sarcoma (malignant tumour) in his leg. He took the news in stride and underwent surgery to have the tumour removed. But then he developed another, and then another — this time on his lungs. He subsequently had seven little tumours taken off his lungs and finally had a recurrence that claimed his life. The cancer was very aggressive, much like Terry Fox experienced, spreading quickly from his legs to his lungs.

Retinoblastoma itself is curable — simply remove the eyes. But it is now known that retinoblastoma children have a statistically higher chance of developing more cancers as they grow older. If you are one of the affected patients, it probably doesn't much matter what the statistical odds are. It is either zero or a hundred percent for you. Unfortunately, our guitar wizard was one of the unlucky statistics.

"I'm in the wrong fifty percent," Jeff Healey said. Ever the optimist, he continued to look on the positive side. "Well, I've had thirty-nine great years — a terrific time. So here comes a bump. Deal with it."

And he did. He was the first to say he had lived a full and happy life, fuller than most. Jeff claimed to have packed into his life what most people could only hope to experience in many lifetimes. On that score he had no regrets.

Jeff's only real regret was leaving his two young children behind and not getting the chance to see Rachel and Derek's accomplishments and who they would grow up to be.

Jeff's father's biggest regret was not being able to "fix it." "As his dad, you know, when something is wrong and I can't fix it … I just felt so helpless."

Jeff with his children, Rachel and Derek, in happier times.

If Bud could have taken the cancer on himself to spare his son, he would gladly have done so. They had come full circle. As Bud had felt helpless to save his infant son's eyesight, now he stood powerless to save his life. But he had taught him well. In today's world, where many seem to have lost perspective on life, to have forgotten the really important things, Jeff always kept his priorities straight. He put family and friends first and remained true to himself throughout his career.

"I have always defined 'success' in my mind, I suppose, as the ability to make a comfortable living while doing something you love to do, if not what you love to do most," Jeff wrote in the liner notes of his album *Mess of Blues*. "But being a 'star' was never … a priority in my life…. So, with that in mind, I made a conscious decision almost a decade ago to break away from a lot of the things I was involved in … and pursue my interest in early jazz and twentieth-century popular American music … this area of music that has always fascinated me."

Jeff with his dad, Bud Healey.

In a video compilation shot throughout the recording of *Mess of Blues*, the CD that was scheduled for release only weeks after Jeff's death, Jeff's joy in music jumps off the screen. He is laughing in almost every scene, head thrown back, face radiating happiness. That's fitting. Jeff always loved to laugh; he was known for it.

"He gave his whole body over to laughter," says long-time friend Rob Quail.

Even on his deathbed, Jeff never dwelled on the negative. As with his life, he faced death with courage and grace. He seemed more worried about the impact on his friends and family. He called musical friends and left his own unique message to get them in to say goodbye: "Hey, I can't get my iPod to work properly. I need help with it. Maybe you can stop by."

After Jeff's last surgery, his dad found his old stuffed elf packed away. Bud carried it to the hospital and presented the old toy to his bed-ridden son.

"Oh! My Elf!" Jeff's face lit up as he felt the familiar figure. He propped Elf on the pillow beside him. And so he had his pal Elf with him through to the end. But at 5:58 p.m., as the afternoon slipped into evening, Jeff Healey died in his father's arms, with his wife, Cristie, holding his hand. The sun hadn't shone that day, as if it had already gone into mourning over the anticipated loss.

A choked-up Bud whispered, "It's okay, son. You can let go. You've done enough."

Jeff let himself slip away, quietly, peacefully.

You are never quite ready for the death of someone you love, even when the death is expected. And everyone's reaction to death is unique. There is no magic formula. And so it was in the tension-filled hospital room as family and friends hurt and grieved, each in the only way they could.

As Jeff's death was anticipated, the press release was prepared in advance and ready to go. Twenty minutes after Jeff died, Richard Flohil got the call from one of Jeff's band members.

"Jeff is in another band now."

Richard planned to send out the press release and head to Hugh's Room, a Toronto music haunt, to listen to music and drown his sorrows. He never made it out the door. The response was overwhelming, profound, and absolutely immediate.

Heartfelt condolences flooded in, mourning the loss of this great Canadian talent. He died too young and left too much great music unplayed. But people live on through our memories of them. They are not forgotten. We recall them in different ways. Jeff touched so many people in his life that he has undoubtedly left a proud legacy to survive through generations.

As eleven-year-old Jade Watson said, "Everyone wants Jeff back. Everyone wants to see Jeff's big smile and his grand laugh. His laugh was so powerful that everyone wanted to be near Jeff. Now Jeff has died, but he will never die in everyone's heart."

Circle of Life

Jeff was born March 25, 1966, at St. Joseph's Hospital on the Queensway in Toronto. As an infant, both surgeries to remove Jeff's eyes were performed at St. Joseph's. Although his music took Jeff all over the world, he ultimately succumbed to cancer, dying at his birthplace, St. Joseph's Hospital, on March 2, 2008.

Things to Think About

As someone who could have had all the excuses to give up, Jeff Healey chose not to. He chose to succeed, to push himself, to see the good in life, to embrace each day. Even after the return of cancer in his last years, Jeff didn't quit. He still played, toured, and recorded until he was physically unable. We all get to make a choice about how we are going to live life each day. Which do you choose? Which will you choose?

Jeff's Greatest Strengths According to His Family and Friends

- His music — that speaks for itself.
- His passion for what he was doing.
- Loyalty.
- Independence.
- Determination.
- Debating — he should have been a lawyer. He could debate anything.
- Public speaking — he could stand up in front of thousands of people.
- Positive attitude.
- Persistence.
- Ability to achieve whatever he set his mind to.
- His love for all kinds of music. He was a musicologist.
- Amazing recall and memory.
- Directions. He was unbelievable and could get anyone out of anywhere.
- Generosity.
- Constant joy.
- Honesty.
- Sense of humour.

Eulogy

At Jeff's funeral service an unlikely collection of people from all walks of life whom Jeff had touched in his life showed up to pay their respects and say goodbye, each in their own way. Jeff's long-time friend and first bandmate, Rob Quail, gave a heartfelt and personal eulogy, speaking about Jeff and celebrating his life. Here is an excerpt from the eulogy that Rob has graciously shared:

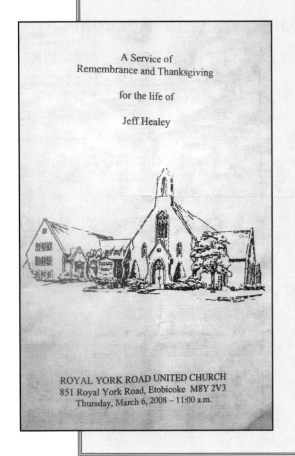

A Service of
Remembrance and Thanksgiving

for the life of

Jeff Healey

ROYAL YORK ROAD UNITED CHURCH
851 Royal York Road, Etobicoke M8Y 2V3
Thursday, March 6, 2008 – 11:00 a.m.

My name is Rob Quail, and I have had the privilege of being a friend of Jeff's since we first met in … I think the year was 1979. Jeff would remember what year it was, and what month, maybe even the day. He was the remembering-details guy. As kids, we thrashed about and made mistakes and learned how to play in bands and went through the experience of falling in love with the process of creating music in that setting. It was a magical time for both of us, and we formed a powerful bond in that period that formed the basis for a friendship that lasted twenty-nine years.

My thought today was to talk about Jeff the person, because so much is already being written about Jeff the musician. But to me these two aspects of him are blurred. If ever there was a person whose art reflected the man, it's Jeff.

Let me explain what I mean. What are the words they are using this week in the media to describe his music?

Direct. There is a directness to Jeff's approach to making music. It's right out there, right to the point, asserts itself, fills the room. Every note is a *big* note. Same with his personality. He never hesitated to offer up his feelings on things when asked, sometimes when not asked. Jeff once explained to me at length, very convincingly I might add, that all post-war styles of jazz were created as part of a great evil conspiracy.

Down to earth. Jeff's taste in music was very down-to-earth: blues and the more direct forms of jazz, the foundations, meat-and-potatoes music. There's a huge parallel there with his tastes for other things in life — beef stew, hamburgers, wearing pajamas at home and T-shirts onstage. My wife remarked to me yesterday that she was astonished to learn that, at the peak of the Healey Band thing, Jeff had a hairstylist. She said she would have liked to have seen that — Jeff having the patience to get his hair done before every show!

Power to move people. For a guy who hasn't had a mainstream record in a couple of decades, his passing sure has attracted a lot of attention. And while much of the mainstream media words have been about the music, I am struck by how many of the emails and bulletin-board posts are about Jeff as a person. He had a manner of speaking to people, getting to know people, sizing them up — the many musical guests at the club on Thursday and anyone in the crowd who approached him. He could make them feel at ease and special and important to him.

Energy. Jeff's playing exuded energy, and so did his way of living. Recently, Jeff and I had a conversation about mortality. Jeff remarked, "You know, Rob, I've experienced more and done more living in my forty-one years than most people do in eighty." And he was right.

This, in a way, though, was the one great contradiction about Jeff. He attracted attention without it always being "Hey, look at me." Jeff was just himself, did what came naturally, and people loved it and loved him. But he was also a very private man, and I can say with certainty that the happiest period in Jeff's life was the last few years when he was able to spend so much time at home with Cristie and his children.

But for me the most powerful aspect of Jeff's music, that was echoed in his life in a way I will describe in a moment, was that it could be stunningly beautiful — his touch on a legato note, his warm vibrato, his moving phrasing. This I see very directly and powerfully translated in Jeff's life in the gentle way he would touch Derek with his hands. I wasn't around them much when Rachel was little, but I got to see a lot of Jeff with Derek, and this big, powerful man moved his hands when he touched his son with such gentleness and tenderness, it never ceased to move me.

I have an anecdote to share in closing. This past Saturday, Jeff was feeling quite weak, and the combination of medications made it difficult for him to focus on what was going on. A few of us were in the room, and Jeff was trying to follow the conversation but was drifting in and out. Soon I announced that my wife, Kath, and I had to leave for the evening, but that we would be back the next morning with some fresh homemade banana bread. Jeff immediately piped up and said, in the strongest voice I had heard from him in a while, the last complete sentence he ever said to me ... "I don't eat banana bread."

I am grateful that we ever met, that we became such great friends, that we went though that fantastic journey of learning together, and most of all that we had the past couple of years to really reconnect. I'm also grateful that we had the chance to play an entire show together late last year. That's a memory that I will always carry with me.

Jeff was absolutely one-of-a-kind. He was his own man, his own special mix of character and talent. And he was a wonderful friend.

Jeff's Life Lessons

When asked what Jeff's life lessons for kids today would be, Jeff's family and friends made the following comments.

Bud Healey: "If you want to be something, concentrate on that. Enjoy your life but concentrate, centre your thought process on what you want to do."

Linda Healey: "Plug along. You can do it. No matter what, if you want it, you can do it. Whatever you're good at, just keep going. You can get through all your obstacles. If you set your mind you can do it."

Laura Healey: "Don't let any disability or setbacks in your life stop you from pursuing your dreams."

Richard Flohil: "Practice makes close to perfect. And it's work. If you're interested in music, listen to all kinds of music. If you're playing, learn to play all kinds of music. I think he might also say, if you're successful, try to keep your feet on the ground, and at a certain point, probably sooner rather than later, settle down and introduce calm into your life."

Rob Quail: "If there's something you want to say, say it. If there's something you want to play, play it. Don't worry if you're good enough, if you're worthy. Just play."

Glen Wade: "Follow your dreams. If there's something you'd really like, just do it. If you're passionate about something, find a way to see it through. Even when you're razzed, always be yourself."

Joe Rockman: "Believe in your own capabilities to achieve what's in your heart."

Randy Bachman: "Don't mess with drugs or alcohol. They will bring you down. Find your passion or your gift and honour it. Everyone is born with a certain something, and if you do it and do it well, you will have a good life."

Cristie Healey: "Make a living doing something you love. To make your way through life doing something that makes you miserable, what's the point? If you have an aspiration to do something, stick to it. Don't lose that. Never let anybody tell you you're not capable of doing something."

ACKNOWLEDGEMENTS

I have always loved music and believe it has the power to inspire great passion and great deeds. I felt compelled to write about Jeff Healey, who will continue to be such a source of inspiration through the story of his life and music. I could not have done it, however, without the generous help of the following.

My heartfelt thanks to Bud Healey, both for being the exceptional parent who gave the world Jeff, but on a more personal note for opening his heart and home and sharing generously, not only of his time, but also of stories and memorabilia that formed the foundation for this book. I hope I did Jeff justice. Thanks, too, to Rose for sharing Bud and encouraging this project. Likewise, thanks to Laura and Linda Healey for sharing their childhoods with me, and in so doing, let me watch Jeff grow into the man who wouldn't back away from his dreams. Lloyd and Bea gave my first taste of anecdotal tidbits about Jeff and reignited my passion about this project.

Cristie Healey braved her still-fragile heart to share her love and life with Jeff. Richard Flohil went above and beyond the call of duty of a publicist. He is a storyteller extraordinaire and helped to shape my story, both in tone and content. Rob Quail and Glen Wade each shared important parts of Jeff's life and gave the book greater depth by generously sharing those moments with me. Joe Rockman was Jeff's family on the road; he gave Jeff structure and a safe harbour. Thanks, Joe, for generously sharing your time and truly poetic insights.

Cheers to the Canadian music industry and to Terry Kelly, Randy Bachman, and Colin James for taking the time to give their feedback about Jeff. Thanks especially to David Wilcox for being the first to graciously respond. I salute Jim Sanders and the dedicated staff and students from the Canadian National Institute for the Blind and thank them for the gift of allowing me a glimpse into their lives and world.

Thanks to Michael Carroll at Dundurn Press, probably the hardest-working editor in Canada, for leading me on this adventure. Thanks, too, to Kendra Marcus and Patrick Boyer for showing interest in the project and encouraging me to persevere. Special thanks to Richard Scrimger, who cared enough to make time to vet an early draft and push me to get the book done.

Where would I be without my friends and family? Sherri Somerville, Sandy Gene, Carin Makuz, and Cathy Wilson all gave valuable input when I most needed it. Dale Castellarin gave me my sightlines and starting point, which made all the difference. Brian Henry and Melody Richardson sparked my interest to start writing again. Thanks to my parents for making me believe I could write long before I really could! Thanks to my ever-supportive and loving husband, Don, and my amazing children, Jade, Chase, and Dakota.

Image Credits

Joe Rockman: Pages 9, 10 (upper), 12

Barrie Wentzell: Page 10 (lower)

Healey Family: Pages 15–69, 82–129

Richard Flohil: Page 71

More Great Dundurn Non-Fiction for Young People

Sergeant Gander
A Canadian Hero
by Robyn Walker
978-1-55488-463-6
$19.99

Sergeant Gander is a fascinating account of the Royal Rifles of Canada's Newfoundland dog mascot and his devotion to duty during the Battle of Hong Kong in the Second World War. Gander fought alongside his fellow Canadian soldiers, armed only with his formidable size, an intimidating set of teeth, and a protective instinct. For his service in battle, Sergeant Gander was awarded the Dickin Medal, which honours animals who display gallantry and devotion to duty in the armed forces. He is the nineteenth dog to receive this award, and the first Canadian canine to do so.

True Stories of Rescue and Survival
Canada's Unknown Heroes
by Carolyn Matthews
978-1-55002-851-5
$19.99

A crab boat off Newfoundland catches fire, and a rescue is undertaken by helicopter. A child goes missing in a New Brunswick forest, and a desperate hunt is mounted. A climber falls on a British Columbia mountain, and a helicopter rescue is attempted. *True Stories of Rescue and Survival* features stories of heroics from across the country, from the past and the present. Its heroes are to be found in the RCMP, city police forces, the Canadian military, and among all the rescue workers and specialists of the Canadian Coast Guard.

Day of the Flying Fox
The True Story of World War II Pilot Charley Fox
by Steve Pitt
978-1-55002-808-9
$19.99

Canadian Second World War Spitfire pilot Charley Fox was noted for his skill in dive bombing and strafing the enemy. On July 17, 1944, while flying over France, he spotted a black staff car, which usually meant a high-ranking Nazi dignitary was a passenger. Fox went into attack the car and has been celebrated as the pilot who seriously wounded German General Erwin Rommel. Steve Pitt focuses on this day in Charley Fox's life, and details fascinating aspects of the period and the conduct of war.

Available at your favourite bookseller.

DUNDURN PRESS
www.dundurn.com

What did you think of this book?
Visit www.dundurn.com for reviews, videos, updates, and more!